FOR ALL ELECTRONIC KEYBOARDS

easy
ELECTRONIC
KEYBOARD
MUSIC®

THE BEST CHRISTMAS SONGS EVER

100

P9-CLX-991

ISBN 0-7935-0897-5

HAL•LEONARD™
CORPORATION

7777 W. BLUEMOUND RD. P.O. BOX 13819 MILWAUKEE, WI 53213

CONTENTS

THE BEST CHRISTMAS SONGS EVER

All I Want For Christmas Is My Two Front Teeth

Regi-Sound Program: 1
Rhythm: Swing or Rock

Words and Music by
Don Gardner

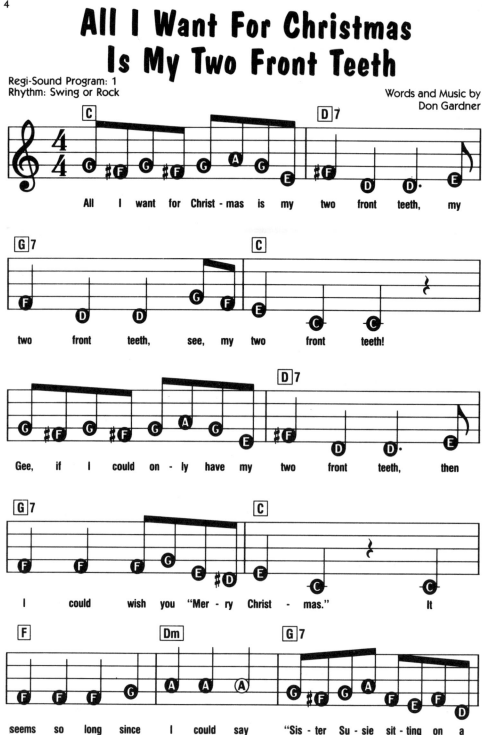

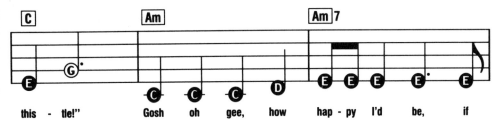

this - tle!"   Gosh   oh   gee,   how   hap - py   I'd   be,   if

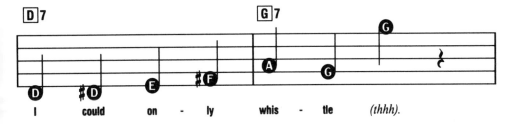

I   could   on - ly   whis - tle   (thhh).

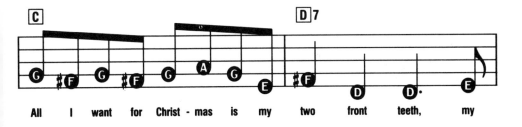

All   I   want   for   Christ - mas   is   my   two   front   teeth,   my

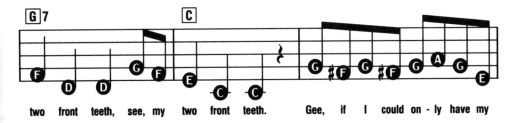

two   front   teeth,   see, my   two   front   teeth.   Gee, if   I   could on - ly have my

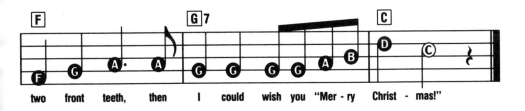

two   front   teeth,   then   I   could   wish   you "Mer - ry   Christ - mas!"

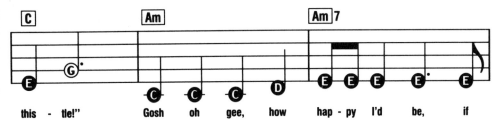

Angels From The Realms Of Glory

Regi-Sound Program: 6
Rhythm: Pops or None

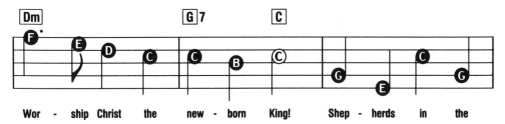

Wor - ship Christ the new - born King! Shep - herds in the

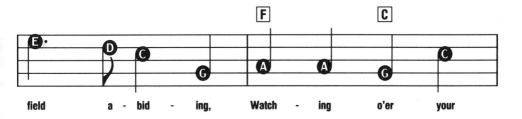

field a - bid - ing, Watch - ing o'er your

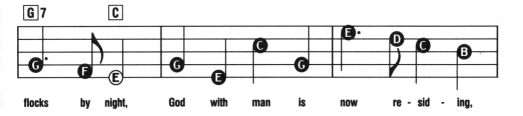

flocks by night, God with man is now re - sid - ing,

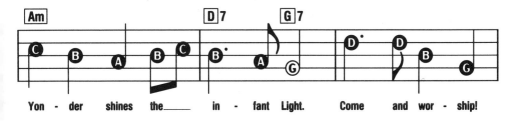

Yon - der shines the_____ in - fant Light. Come and wor - ship!

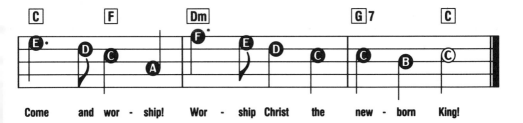

Come and wor - ship! Wor - ship Christ the new - born King!

Angels We Have Heard On High

Regi-Sound Program: 3
Rhythm: Pops or None

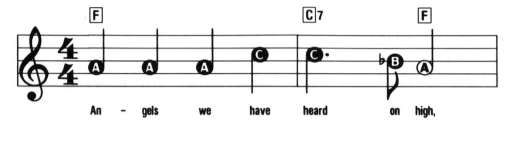

An - gels we have heard on high,

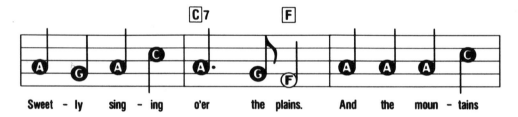

Sweet - ly sing - ing o'er the plains. And the moun - tains

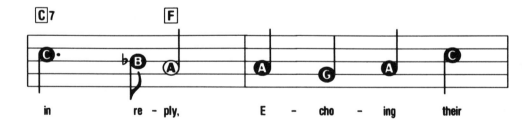

in re - ply, E - cho - ing their

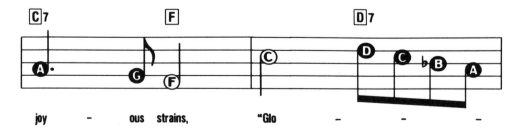

joy - ous strains, "Glo - - -

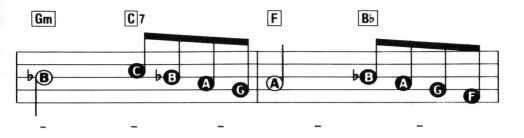

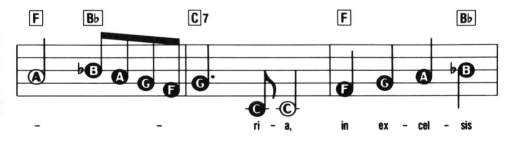

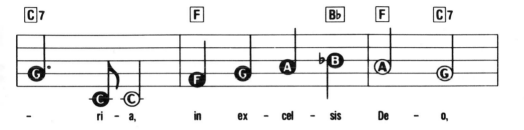

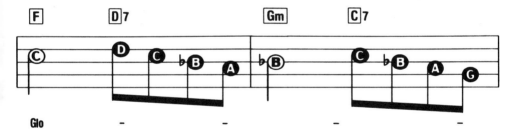

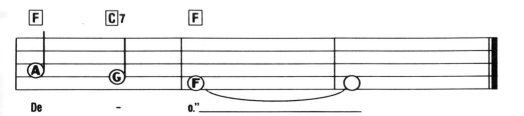

Auld Lang Syne

Regi-Sound Program: 2
Rhythm: March, Fox-Trot or Pops

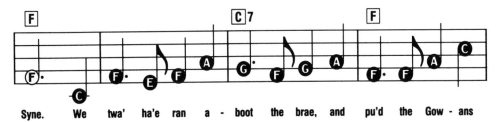

Syne. We twa' ha'e ran a - boot the brae, and pu'd the Gow - ans

fine. We've wand - ered mo - ny a wear - y foot sin

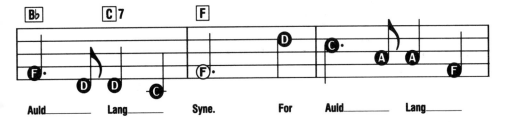

Auld Lang Syne. For Auld Lang

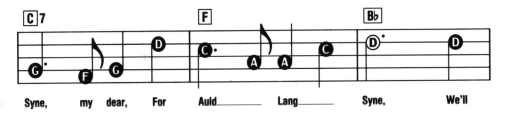

Syne, my dear, For Auld Lang Syne, We'll

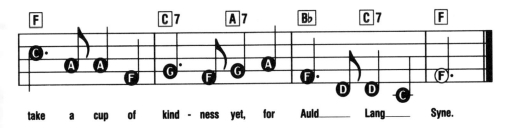

take a cup of kind - ness yet, for Auld Lang Syne.

Away In A Manger

Regi-Sound Program: 1
Rhythm: Waltz

Luther/Spillman

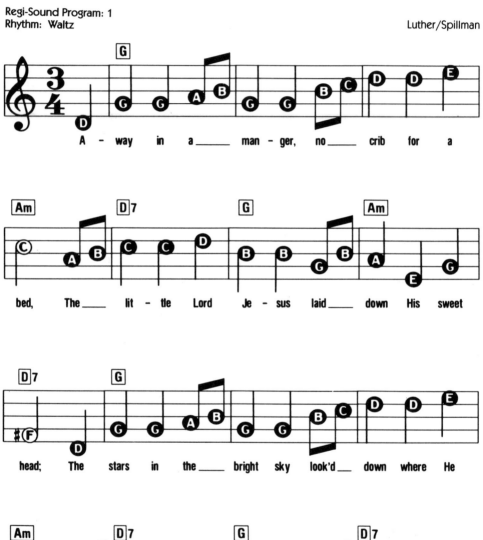

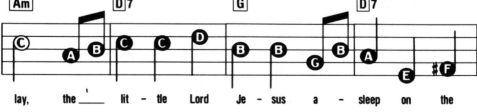

13

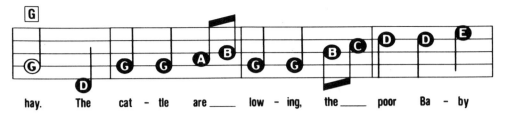

hay. The cat - tle are ___ low - ing, the ___ poor Ba - by

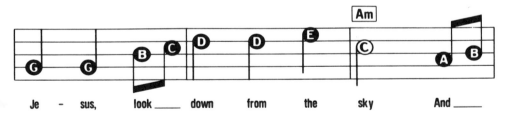

wakes, but ___ lit - tle Lord Je - sus, no ___

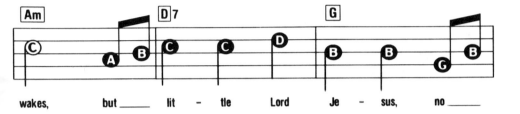

cry - ing He makes. I love Thee, Lord ___

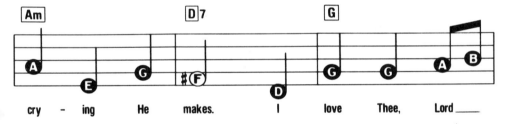

Je - sus, look ___ down from the sky And ___

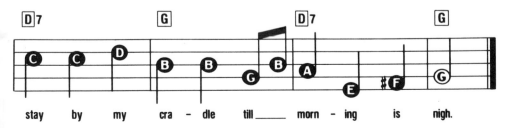

stay by my cra - dle till ___ morn - ing is nigh.

Away In A Manger

Regi-Sound Program: 1
Rhythm: Waltz

Mueller

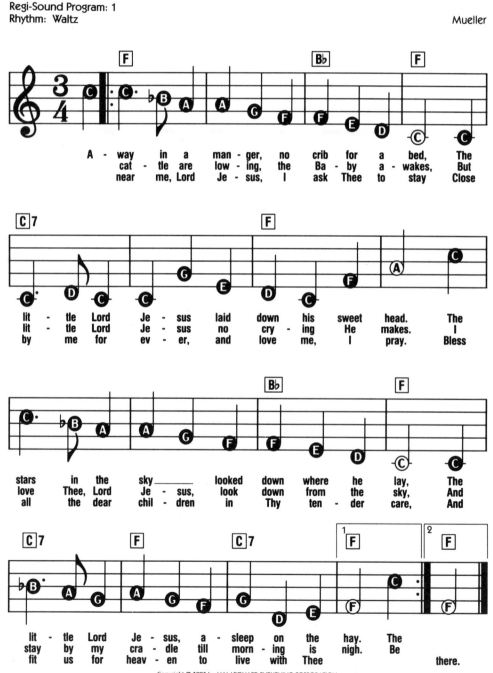

Because It's Christmas

Regi-Sound Program: 2
Rhythm: Swing

Music by Barry Manilow
Lyric by Bruce Sussman and Jack Feldman

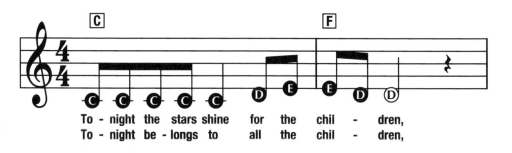

To - night the stars shine for the chil - dren,
To - night be - longs to all the chil - dren,

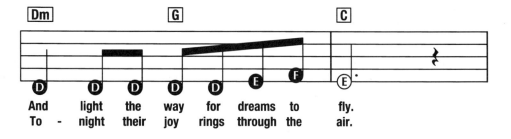

And light the way for dreams to fly.
To - night their joy rings through the air.

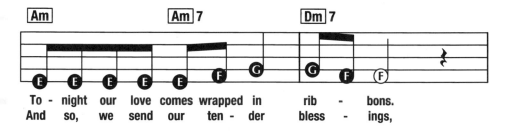

To - night our love comes wrapped in rib - bons.
And so, we send our ten - der bless - ings,

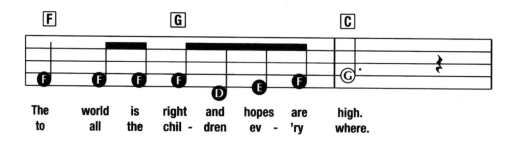

The   world   is   right   and   hopes   are   high.
to   all   the   chil - dren   ev - 'ry   where.

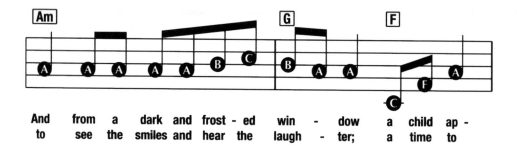

And   from   a   dark   and   frost - ed   win   -   dow   a   child   ap -
to   see   the   smiles   and   hear   the   laugh   -   ter;   a   time   to

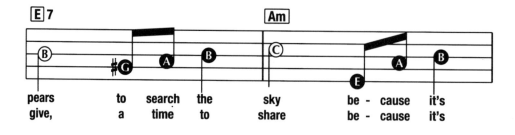

pears   to   search   the   sky   be - cause   it's
give,   a   time   to   share   be - cause   it's

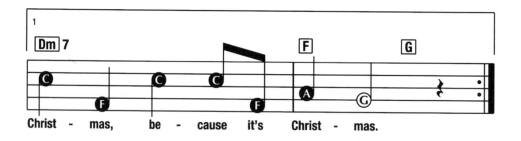

Christ - mas,   be - cause   it's   Christ - mas.

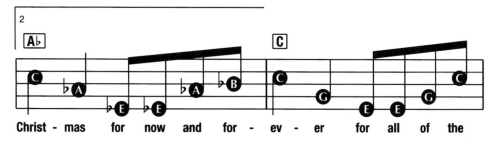

Christ - mas for now and for - ev - er for all of the

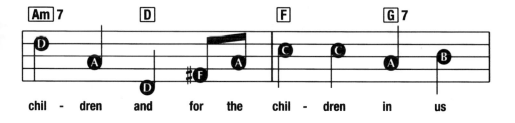

chil - dren and for the chil - dren in us

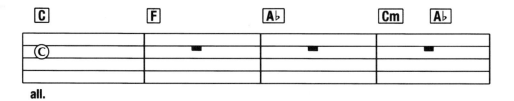

all.

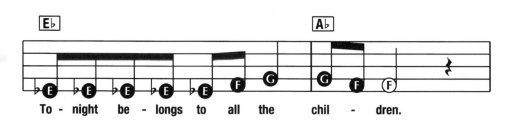

To - night be - longs to all the chil - dren.

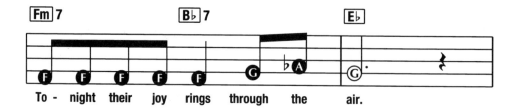

To - night their joy rings through the air.

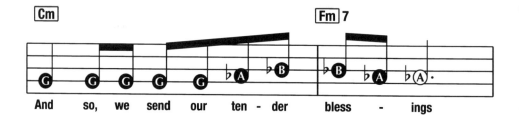

And so, we send our ten - der bless - ings

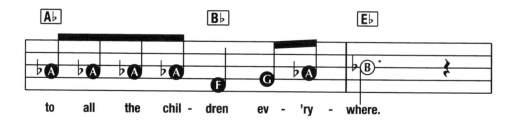

to all the chil - dren ev - 'ry - where.

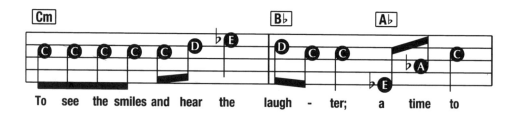

To see the smiles and hear the laugh - ter; a time to

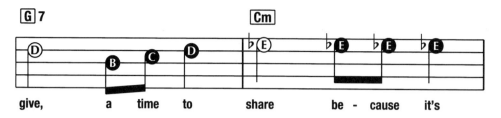

give, a time to share be - cause it's

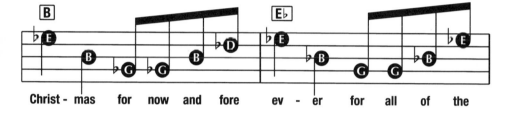

Christ - mas for now and fore ev - er for all of the

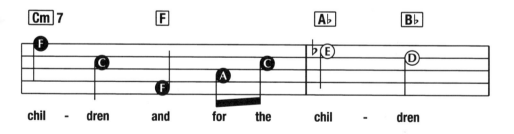

chil - dren and for the chil - dren

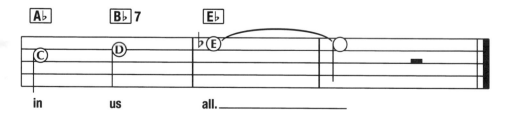

in us all._____

Blue Christmas

Regi-Sound Program: 3
Rhythm: Fox Trot or Swing

Words and Music by Billy Hayes
and Jay Johnson

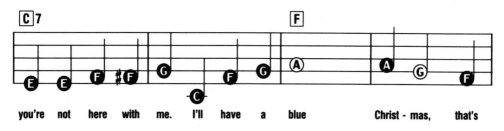

you're not here with me. I'll have a blue Christ - mas, that's

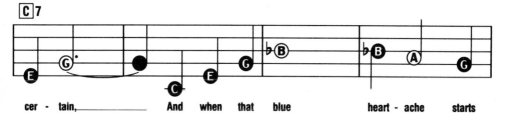

cer - tain,_____ And when that blue heart - ache starts

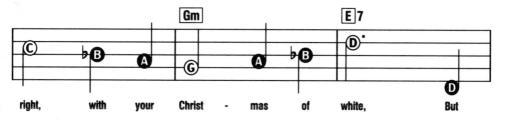

hurt - in',_____ You'll be do - in' all

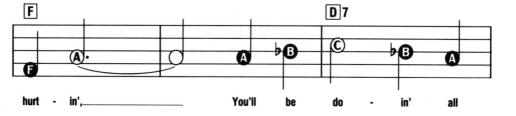

right, with your Christ - mas of white, But

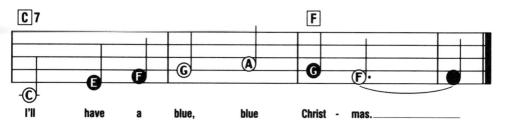

I'll have a blue, blue Christ - mas._____

Bring A Torch, Jeannette, Isabella

Regi-Sound Program: 3
Rhythm: Waltz

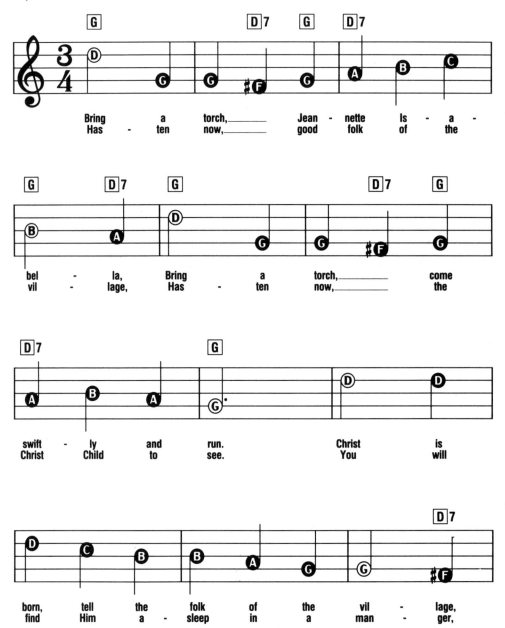

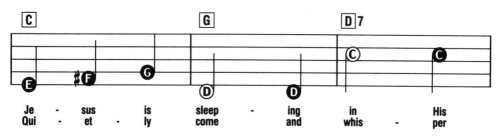

Je - sus is sleep - ing in His
Qui - et - ly come and in whis - per

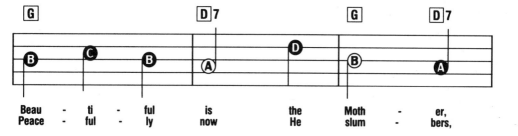

cra - dle, Ah, ah,
soft - ly, Hush, hush,

Beau - ti - ful is the Moth - er,
Peace - ful - ly now the He slum - bers,

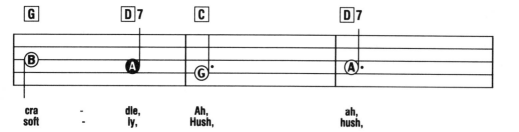

Ah, ah, Beau - ti - ful is her
Hush, hush, Peace - ful - ly now He

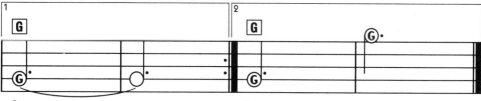

Son._____ sleeps.

The Chipmunk Song

Regi-Sound Program: 3
Rhythm: Waltz

Words and Music by
Ross Bagdasarian

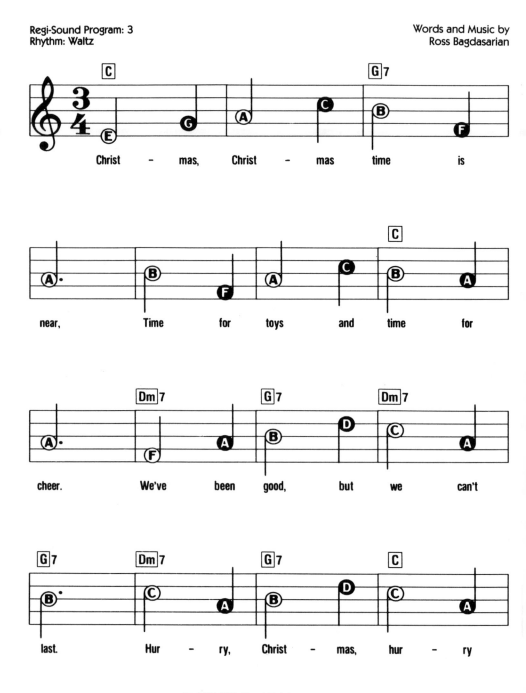

25

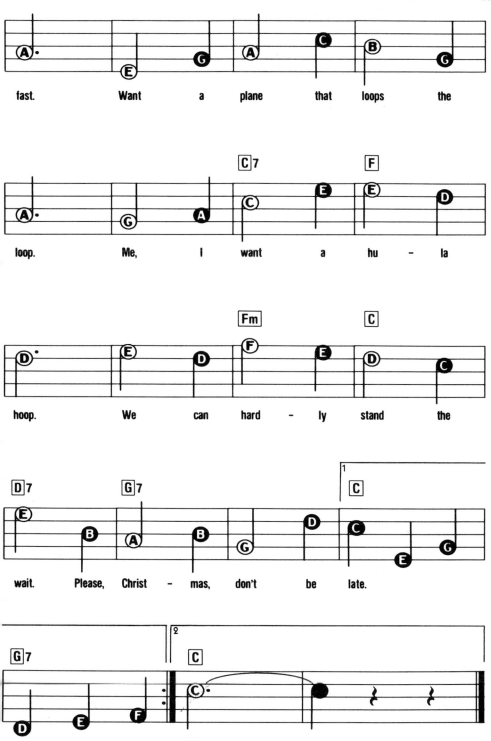

fast.   Want   a   plane   that   loops   the

loop.   Me,   I   want   a   hu – la

hoop.   We   can   hard – ly   stand   the

wait.   Please,   Christ – mas,   don't   be   late.

late. _____

Christ Was Born On Christmas Day

Regi-Sound Program: 6
Rhythm: 6/8 March or Waltz

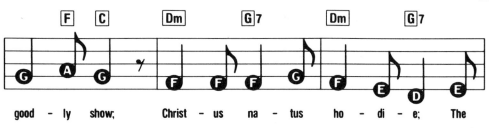

good - ly show; Christ - us na - tus ho - di - e; The

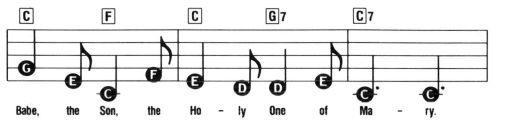

Babe, the Son, the Ho - ly One of Ma - ry.

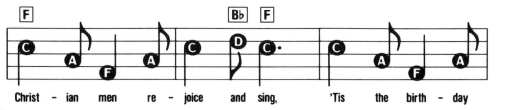

Christ - ian men re - joice and sing, 'Tis the birth - day

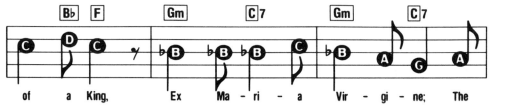

of a King, Ex Ma - ri - a Vir - gi - ne; The

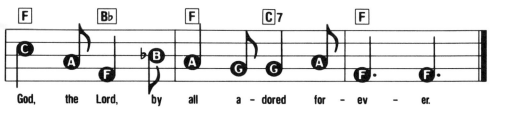

God, the Lord, by all a - dored for - ev - er.

C-H-R-I-S-T-M-A-S

Regi-Sound Program: 5
Rhythm: Fox Trot or Ballad

Words by Jenny Lou Carson
Music by Eddy Arnold

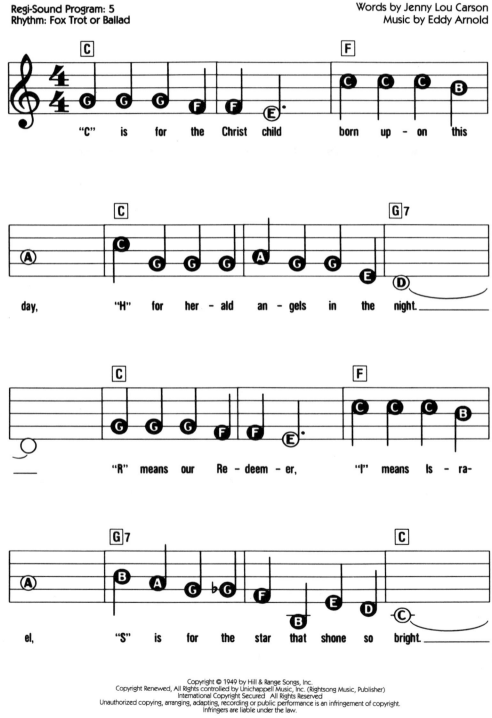

29

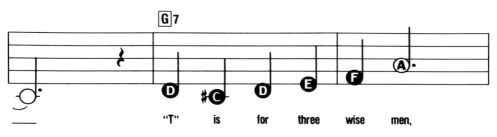

"T" is for three wise men,

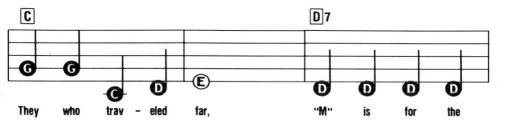

They who trav – eled far, "M" is for the

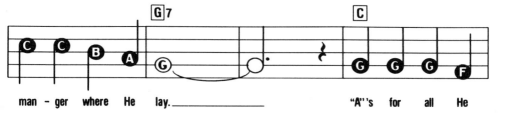

man – ger where He lay._____ "A"'s for all He

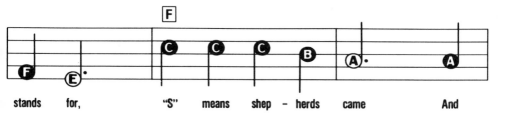

stands for, "S" means shep – herds came And

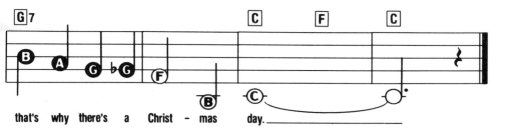

that's why there's a Christ – mas day._____

Christmas Is

Regi-Sound Program: 10
Rhythm: Fox Trot or Slow Swing

Lyrics by Spence Maxwell
Music by Percy Faith

The Coventry Carol

Regi-Sound Program: 1
Rhythm: Waltz

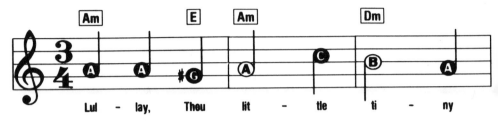

Lul - lay, Thou lit - tle ti - ny

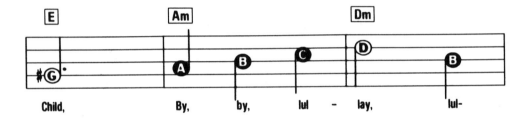

Child, By, by, lul - lay, lul-

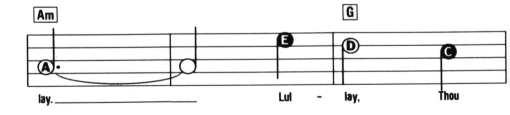

lay. _____ Lul - lay, Thou

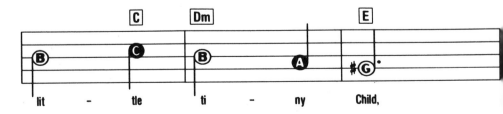

lit - tle ti - ny Child,

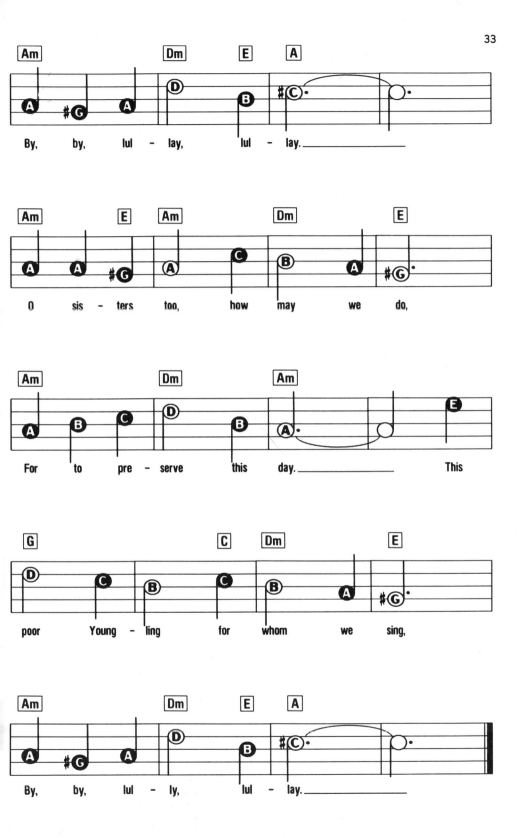

The Christmas Waltz

Regi-Sound Program: 5
Rhythm: Waltz

Words by Sammy Cahn
Music by Jule Styne

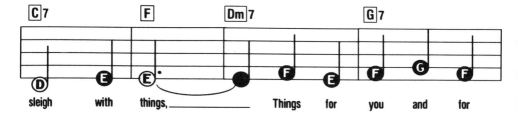

Frost - ed win - dow panes,_____ can - dles gleam - ing in-

side, paint - ed can - dy canes_____ on the tree;

San - ta's on his way, he's filled his

sleigh with things,_____ Things for you and for

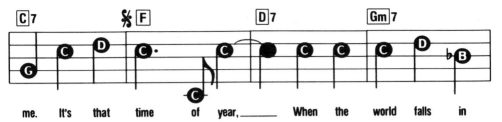

me. It's that time of year,_____ When the world falls in

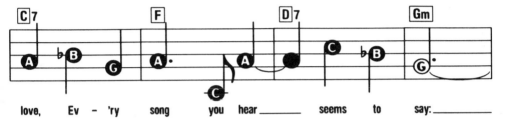

love, Ev – 'ry song you hear_____ seems to say:_____

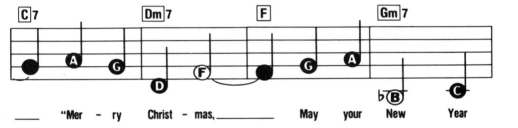

_____ "Mer – ry Christ – mas,_____ May your New Year

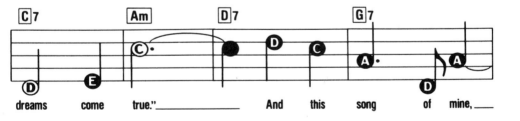

dreams come true."_____ And this song of mine, ____

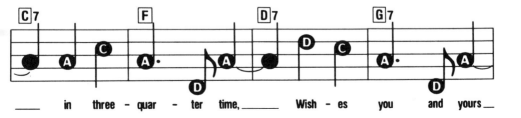

_____ in three – quar – ter time,_____ Wish – es you and yours __

36

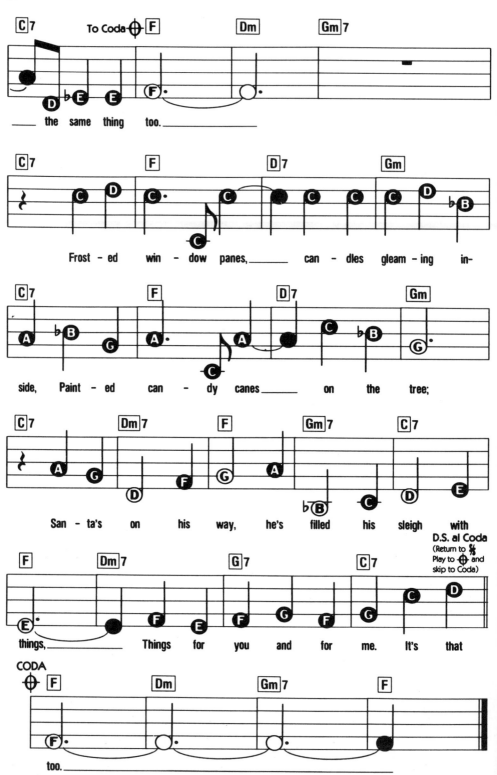

Deck The Hall

Regi-Sound Program: 5
Rhythm: March, Polka or Pops

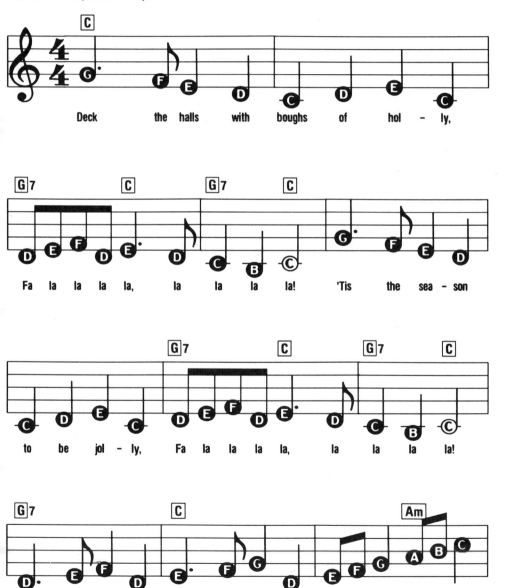

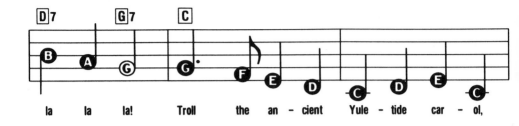

la   la   la!   Troll   the   an – cient   Yule – tide   car – ol,

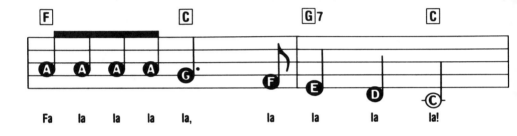

Fa   la   la   la   la,   la   la   la   la!

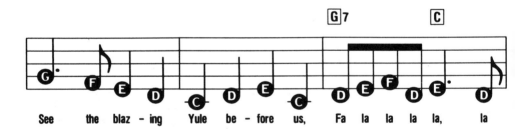

See   the   blaz – ing   Yule   be – fore   us,   Fa   la   la   la   la,   la

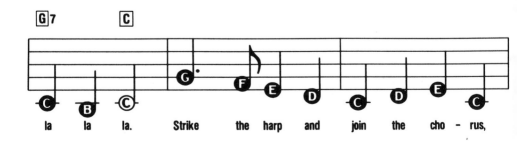

la   la   la.   Strike   the   harp   and   join   the   cho – rus,

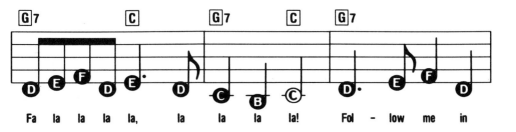

Fa la la la la, la la la la! Fol - low me in

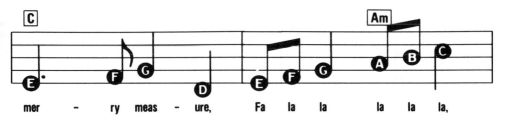

mer - ry meas - ure, Fa la la la la la, la

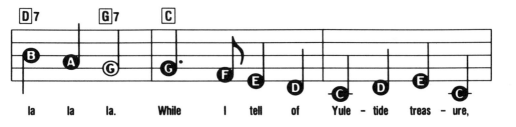

la la la. While I tell of Yule - tide treas - ure,

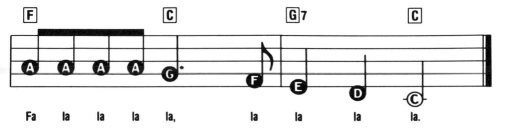

Fa la la la la, la la la la.

Do They Know It's Christmas?

Regi-Sound Program: 1
Rhythm: Latin or Rock

Words and Music by M. Ure
and B. Geldof

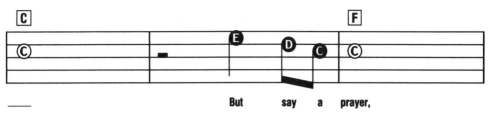

But say a prayer,

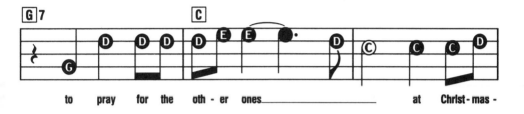

to pray for the oth - er ones_____ at Christ - mas -

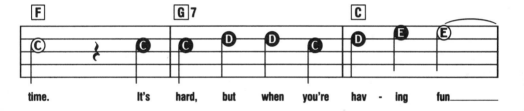

time. It's hard, but when you're hav - ing fun_____

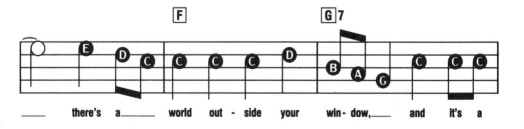

_____ there's a_____ world out - side your win - dow,_____ and it's a

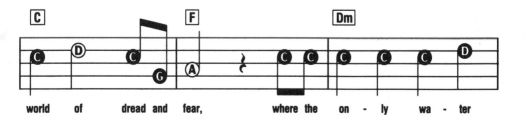

world of dread and fear, where the on - ly wa - ter

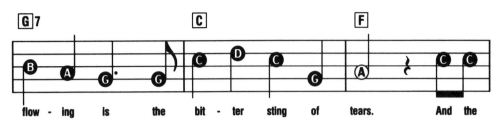

flow - ing   is   the   bit - ter   sting   of   tears.   And   the

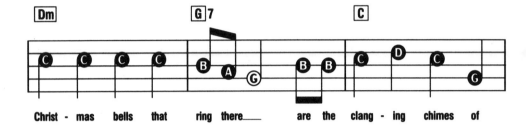

Christ - mas   bells   that   ring there____   are   the   clang - ing   chimes   of

doom.   Well, to - night   thank   God   it's   them   in - stead   of

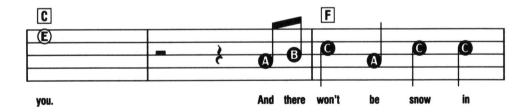

you.   And   there   won't   be   snow   in

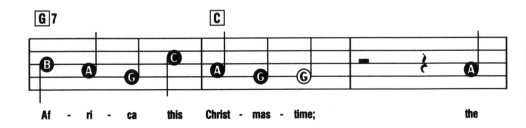

Af - ri - ca   this   Christ - mas - time;   the

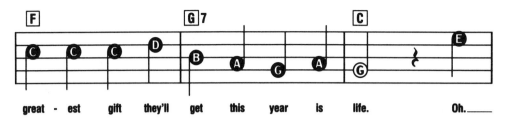

great - est gift they'll get this year is life. Oh.____

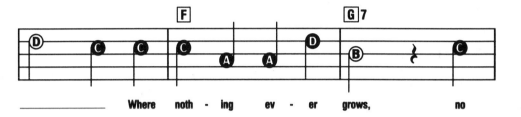

_____ Where noth - ing ev - er grows, no

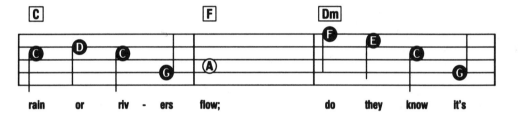

rain or riv - ers flow; do they know it's

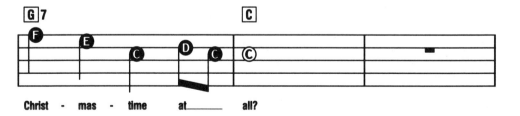

Christ - mas - time at____ all?

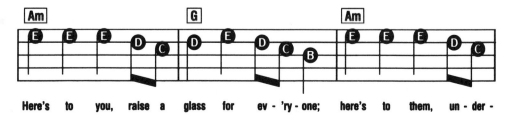

Here's to you, raise a glass for ev - 'ry - one; here's to them, un - der-

44

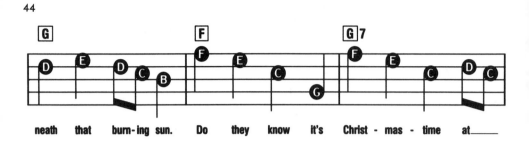

neath that burn-ing sun. Do they know it's Christ - mas - time at___

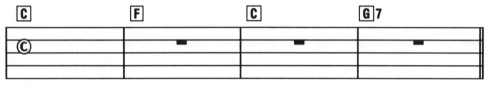

all?

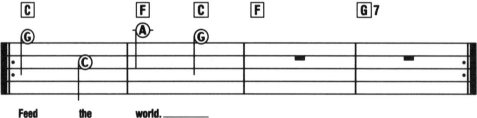

Feed the world._____

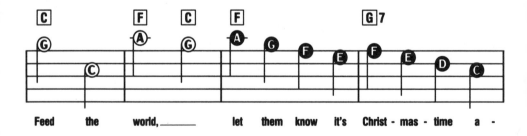

Feed the world,_____ let them know it's Christ - mas - time a -

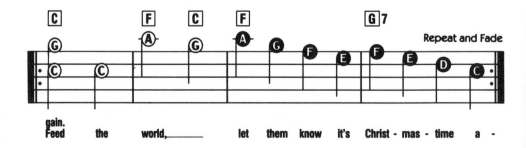

gain.
Feed the world,_____ let them know it's Christ - mas - time a -

Do You Hear What I Hear

Regi-Sound Program: 4
Rhythm: 8 Beat or Pops

Words and Music by Noel Regney
and Gloria Shayne

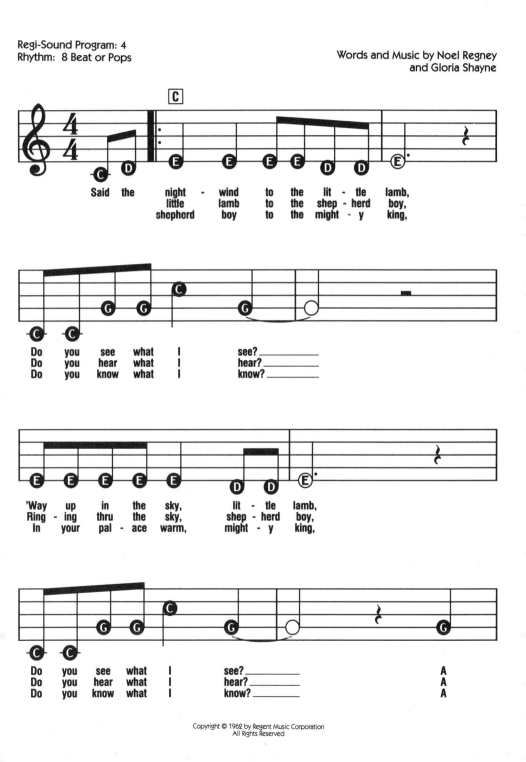

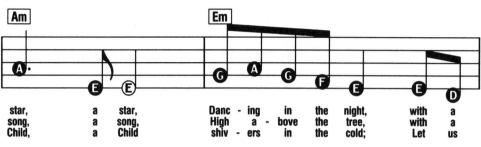

star,   a   star,   Danc - ing   in   the   night,   with   a
song,   a   song,   High   a - bove   the   tree,   with   a
Child,   a   Child   shiv - ers   in   the   cold;   Let   us

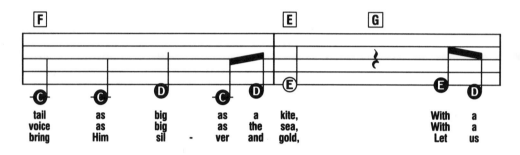

tail   as   big   as   a   kite,   With   a
voice   as   big   as   the   sea,   With   a
bring   Him   sil - ver   and   gold,   Let   us

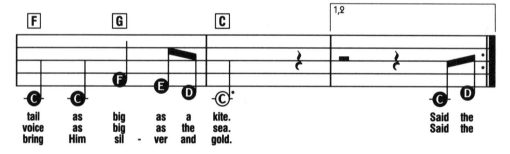

tail   as   big   as   a   kite.   Said   the
voice   as   big   as   the   sea.   Said   the
bring   Him   sil - ver   and   gold.

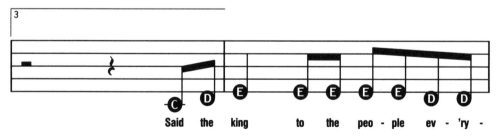

Said   the   king   to   the   peo - ple   ev - 'ry -

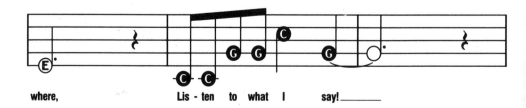

where,   Lis - ten   to   what   I   say!_____

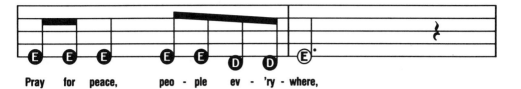

Pray for peace, peo - ple ev - 'ry - where,

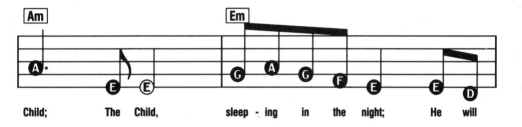

Lis - ten to what I say!_____ The

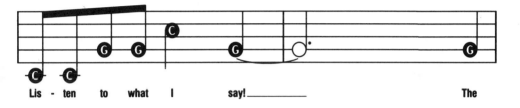

Child; The Child, sleep - ing in the night; He will

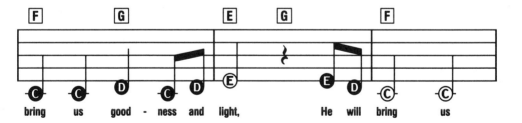

bring us good - ness and light, He will bring us

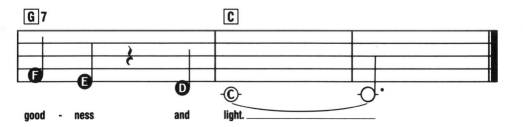

good - ness and light._____

The First Noel

Regi-Sound Program: 9
Rhythm: Waltz

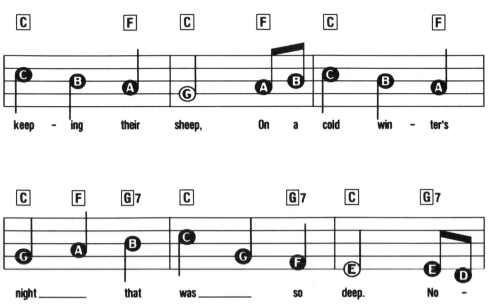

keep - ing their sheep, On a cold win - ter's

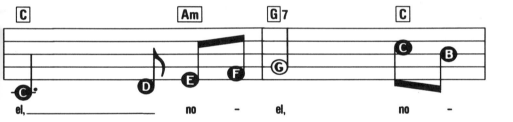

night _____ that was _____ so deep. No -

el, _____ no - el, no -

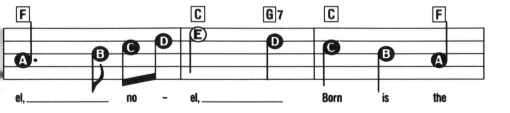

el, _____ no - el, _____ Born is the

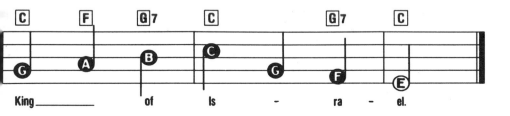

King _____ of Is - ra - el.

The Friendly Beasts

Regi-Sound Program: 3
Rhythm: Waltz

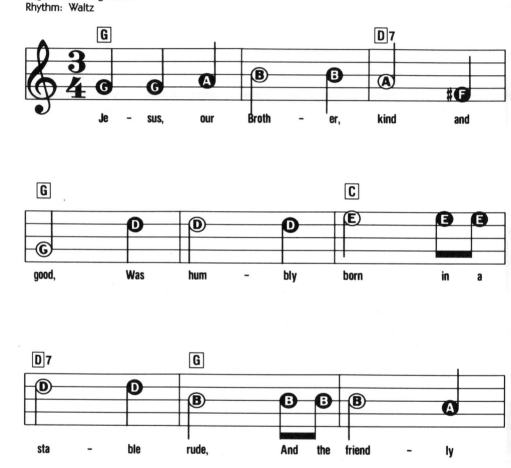

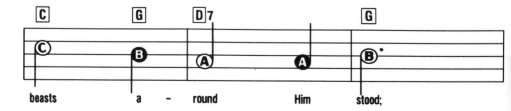

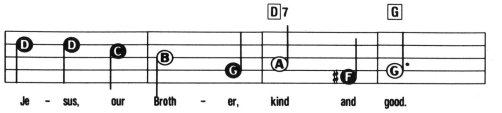

Je – sus, our Broth – er, kind and good.

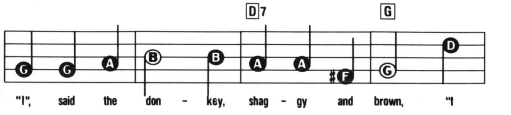

"I", said the don – key, shag – gy and brown, "I

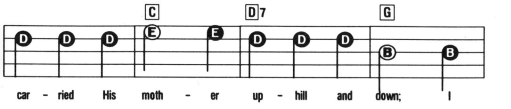

car – ried His moth – er up – hill and down; I

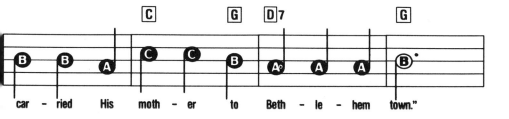

car – ried His moth – er to Beth – le – hem town."

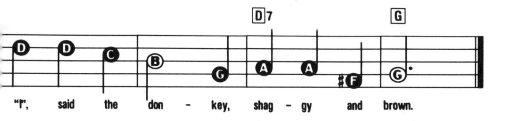

"I", said the don – key, shag – gy and brown.

Frosty The Snow Man

Regi-Sound Program: 2
Rhythm: Fox Trot or March

Words and Music by Steve Nelson
and Jack Rollins

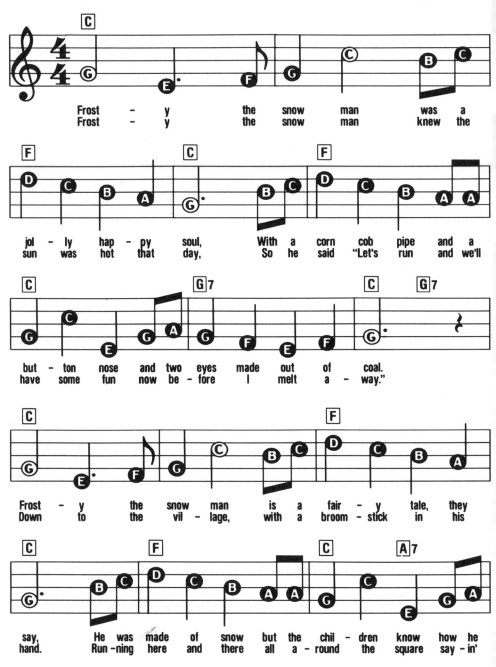

53

Feliz Navidad

Regi-Sound Program: 1
Rhythm: Latin or Bossa Nova

Words and Music by
Jose Feliciano

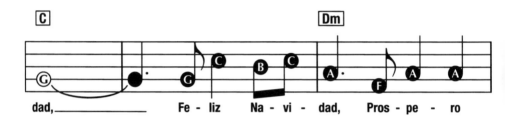

Fe - liz Na - vi - dad, _____ Fe - liz Na - vi -

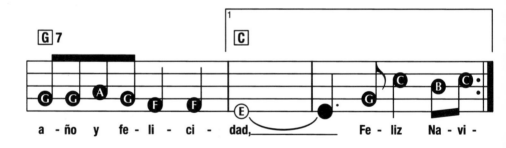

dad, _____ Fe - liz Na - vi - dad, Pros - pe - ro

a - ño y fe - li - ci - dad, _____ Fe - liz Na - vi -

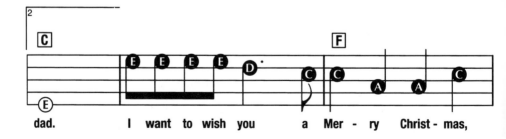

dad. I want to wish you a Mer - ry Christ - mas,

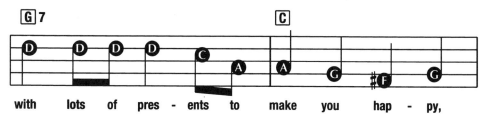

with   lots   of   pres - ents   to   make   you   hap - py,

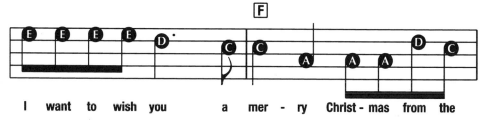

I   want   to   wish   you   a   mer - ry   Christ - mas   from   the

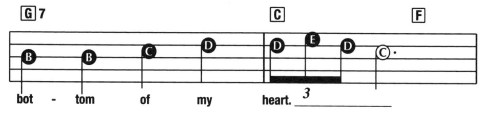

bot - tom   of   my   heart. _____

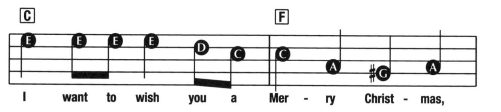

I   want   to   wish   you   a   Mer - ry   Christ - mas,

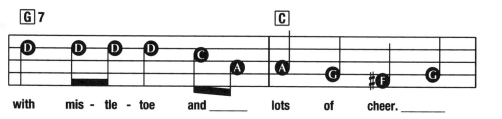

with   mis - tle - toe   and _____   lots   of   cheer. _____

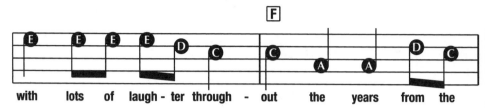

with lots of laugh - ter through - out the years from the

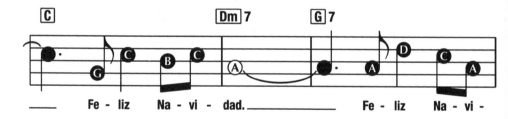

bot - tom of my heart.

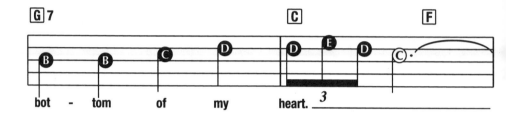

Fe - liz Na - vi - dad. Fe - liz Na - vi -

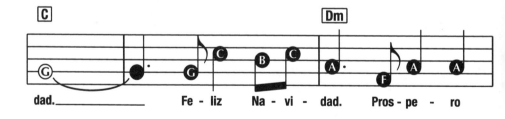

dad. Fe - liz Na - vi - dad. Pros - pe - ro

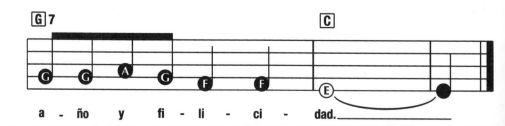

a - ño y fi - li - ci - dad.

Grandma Got Run Over By A Reindeer

Regi-Sound Program: 2
Rhythm: Swing

Words and Music by
Randy Brooks

58

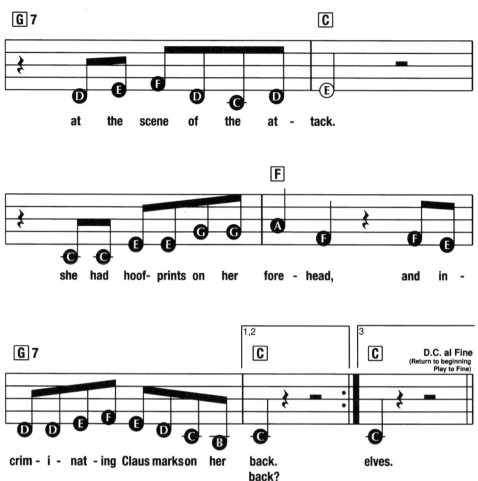

at the scene of the at - tack.

she had hoof- prints on her fore - head, and in -

crim - i - nat - ing Claus marks on her back.
back?

elves.

Additional Lyrics

2. Now we're all so proud of Grandpa,
   He's been taking this so well.
   See him in there watching football,
   Drinking beer and playing cards with Cousin Mel.
   It's not Christmas without Grandma.
   All the family's dressed in black,
   And we just can't help but wonder:
   Should we open up her gifts or send them back? *(To Chorus:)*

3. Now the goose is on the table,
   And the pudding made of fig,
   And the blue and silver candles,
   That would just have matched the hair in Grandma's wig.
   I've warned all my friends and neighbors,
   Better watch out for yourselves.
   They should never give a license
   To a man who drives a sleigh and plays with elves. *(To Chorus:)*

Giving (Santa's Theme)

Regi-Sound Program: 2
Rhythm: Fox Trot or Swing

Music by Henry Mancini
Lyrics by Leslie Bricusse

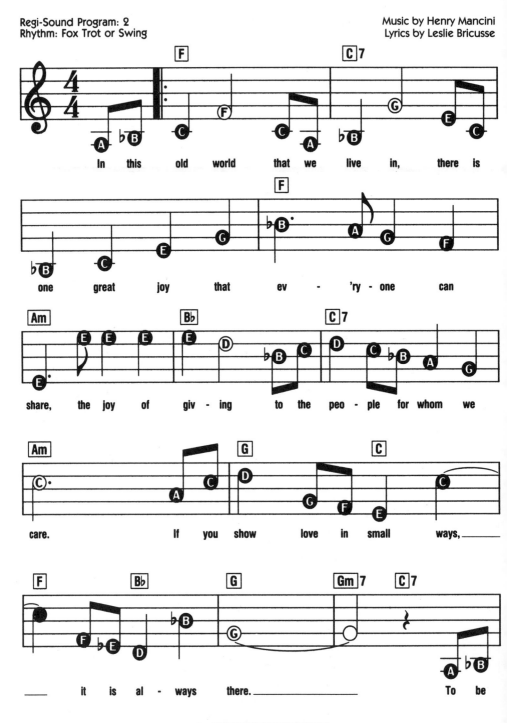

61

God Rest Ye Merry, Gentlemen

Regi-Sound Program: 6
Rhythm: Polka, March or Fox-Trot

63

Good Christian Men, Rejoice

Regi-Sound Program: 6
Rhythm: Waltz

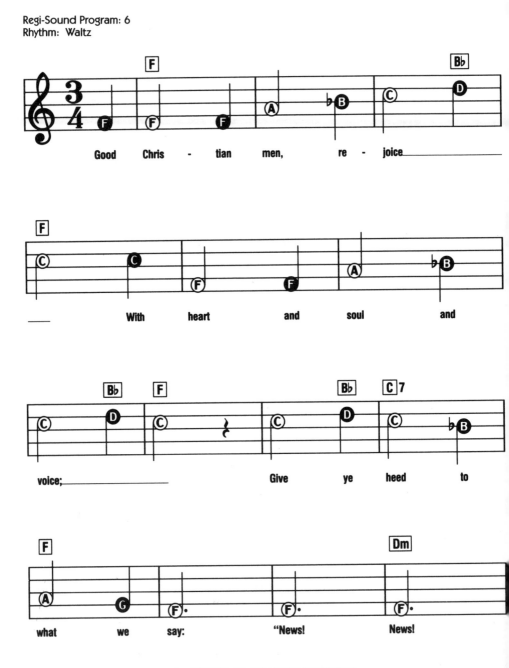

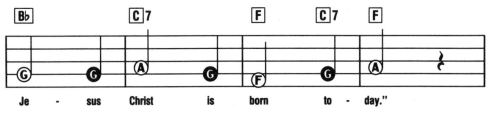

Je - sus Christ is born to - day."

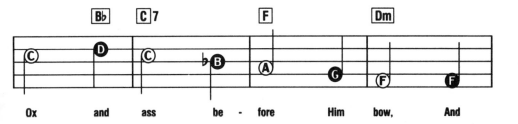

Ox and ass be - fore Him bow, And

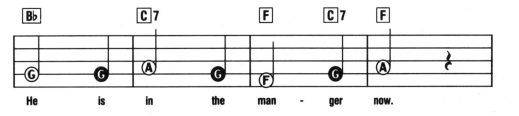

He is in the man - ger now.

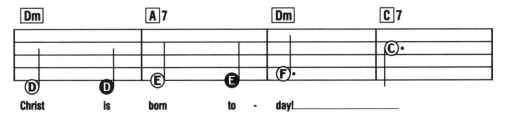

Christ is born to - day!_____

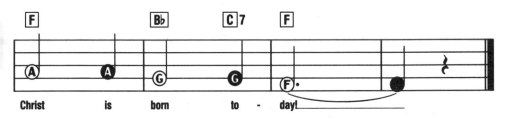

Christ is born to - day!_____

Good King Wenceslas

Regi-Sound Program: 4
Rhythm: Pops, March or Fox-Trot

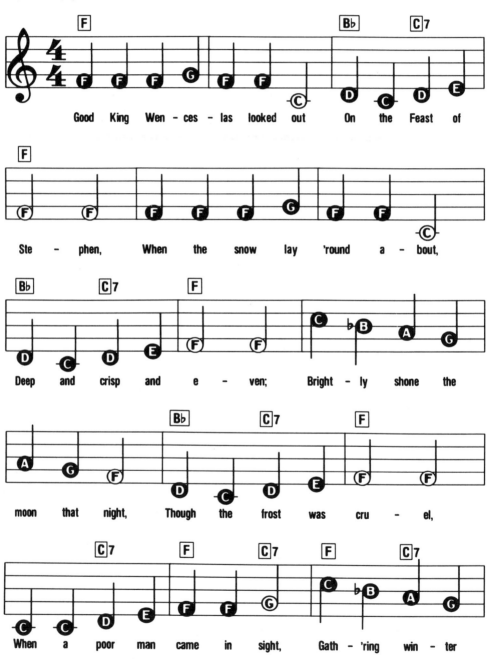

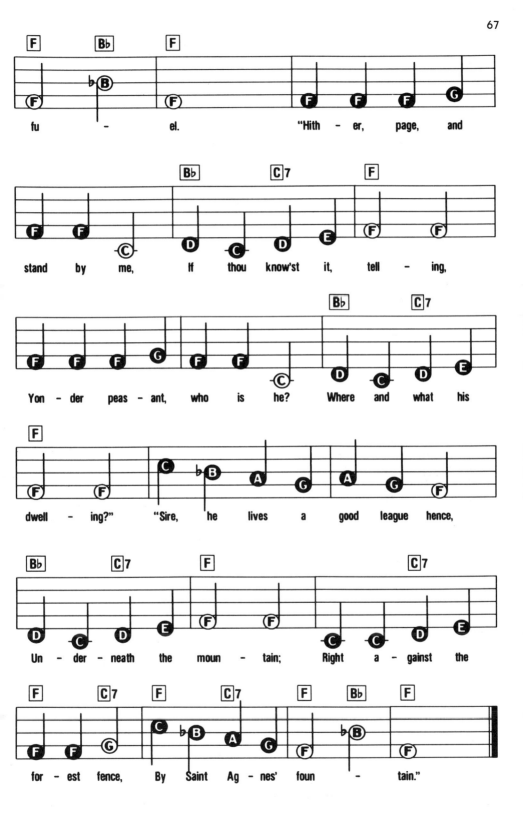

The Greatest Gift Of All

Regi-Sound Program: 4
Rhythm: Shuffle or Country

Words and Music by
John Jarvis

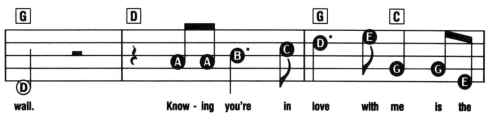

wall.   Know - ing you're in love with me is the

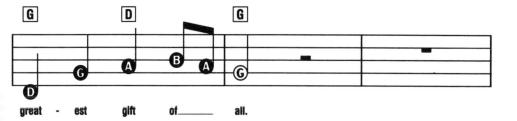

great - est gift of_____ all.

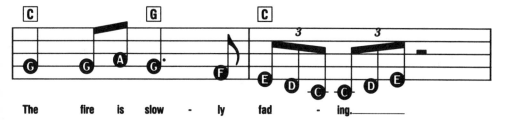

The   fire is slow - ly fad - ing._____

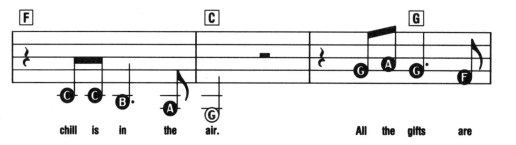

chill is in the air.   All the gifts are

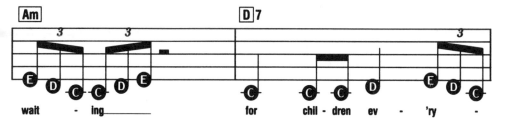

wait - ing_____   for chil - dren ev - 'ry -

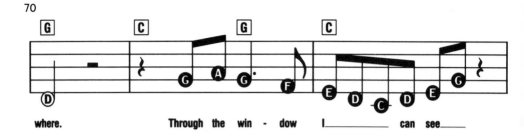

where. Through the win - dow I can see

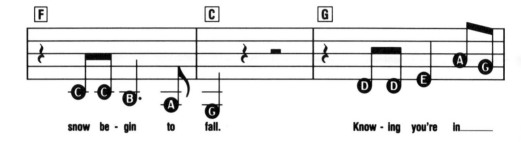

snow be - gin to fall. Know - ing you're in

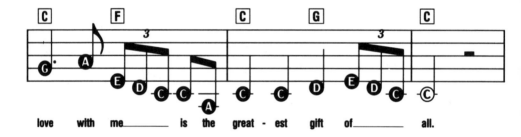

love with me is the great - est gift of all.

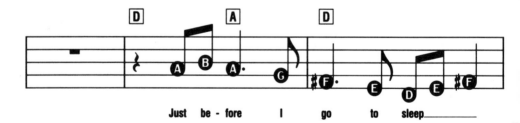

Just be - fore I go to sleep

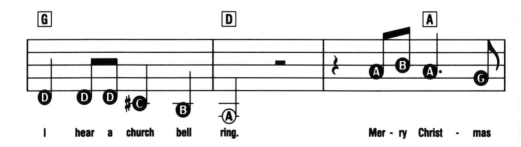

I hear a church bell ring. Mer - ry Christ - mas

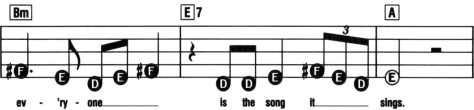

ev - 'ry - one_____ is the song it_____ sings.

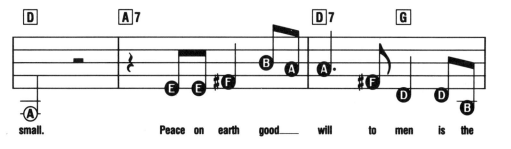

So I say a si - lent prayer_____ for crea - tures great and

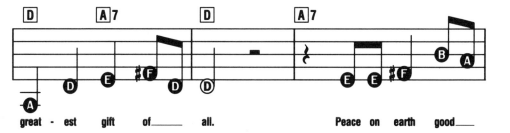

small. Peace on earth good___ will to men is the

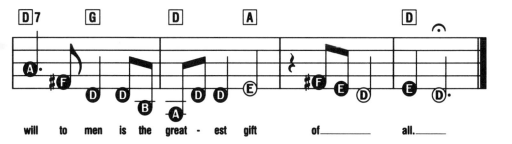

great - est gift of_____ all. Peace on earth good___

D7   G   D   A   D

will to men is the great - est gift of_____ all._____

Hard Candy Christmas

Regi-Sound Program: 4
Rhythm: Country or Shuffle

Words and Music by
Carol Hall

MCA music publishing

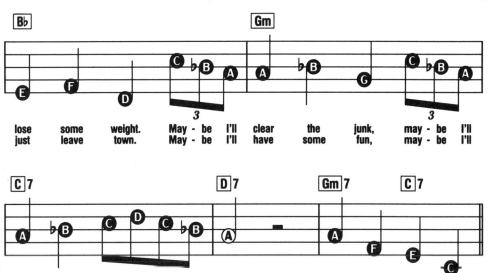

lose some weight. May - be I'll clear the junk, may - be I'll
just leave town. May - be I'll have some fun, may - be I'll

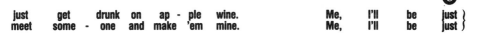

just get drunk on ap - ple wine. Me, I'll be just }
meet some - one and make 'em mine. Me, I'll be just }

fine and dan - dy. Lord, it's like a hard can - dy

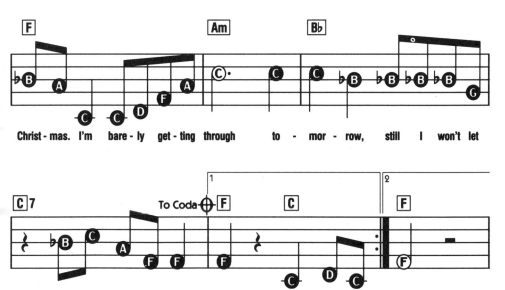

Christ - mas. I'm bare - ly get - ting through to - mor - row, still I won't let

sor - row bring me way down. I'll be____ down.

74

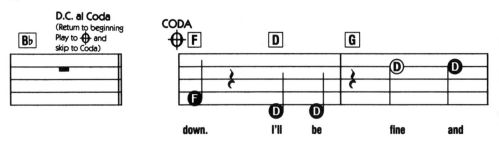

down.   I'll   be   fine   and

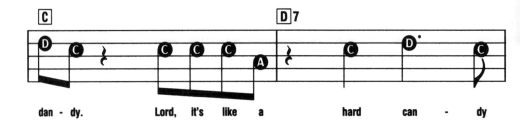

dan - dy.   Lord, it's like a   hard can - dy

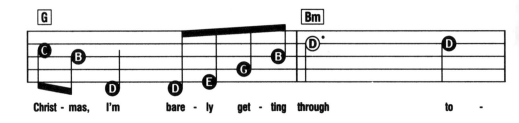

Christ - mas, I'm bare - ly get - ting through   to -

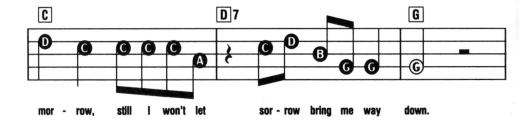

mor - row, still I won't let   sor - row bring me way down.

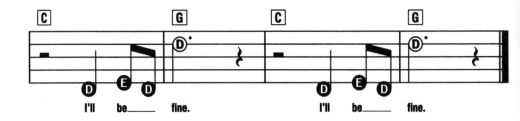

I'll be____ fine.   I'll be____ fine.

Have Yourself A Merry Little Christmas

Regi-Sound Program: 7
Rhythm: Swing or Big Band

By Ralph Blane
and Hugh Martin

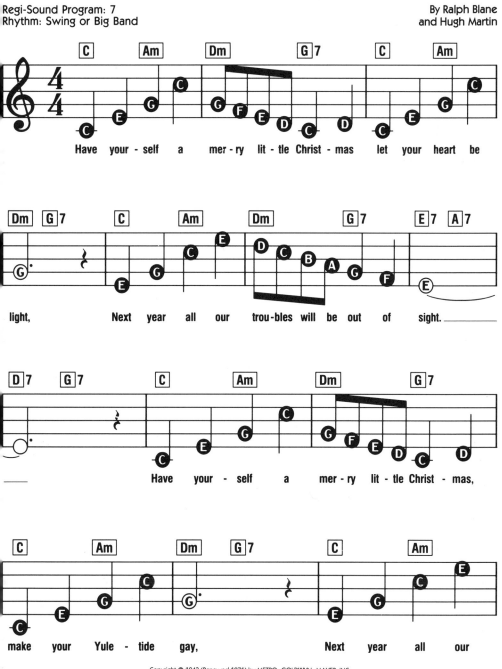

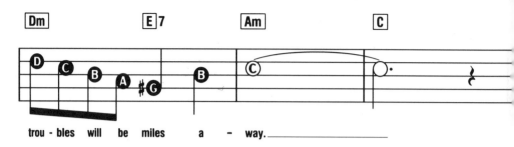

trou - bles will be miles a - way._____

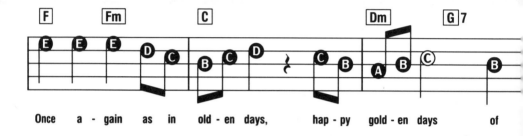

Once a - gain as in old - en days, hap - py gold - en days of

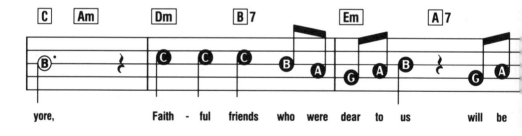

yore, Faith - ful friends who were dear to us will be

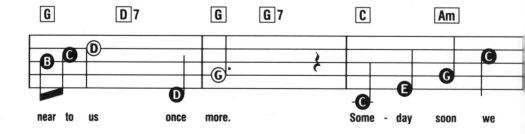

near to us once more. Some - day soon we

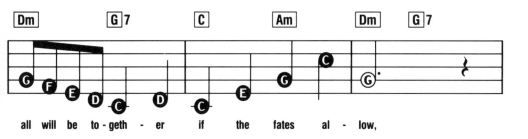

all will be to-geth - er if the fates al - low,

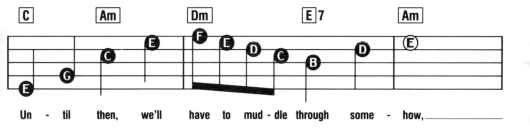

Un - til then, we'll have to mud-dle through some - how,_____

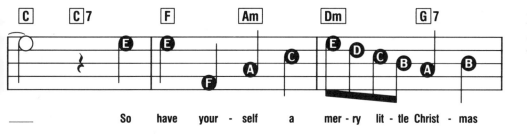

_____ So have your - self a mer - ry lit - tle Christ - mas

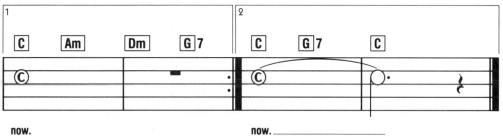

now.   now._____

77

Hark! The Herald Angels Sing

Regi-Sound Program: 5
Rhythm: March, Pops or None

79

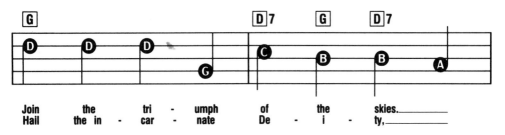

Join the tri - umph of the skies._____
Hail the in - car - nate De - i - ty,_____

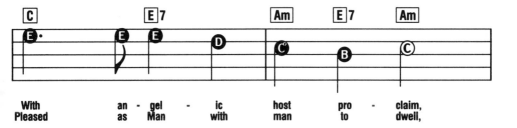

With an - gel - ic host pro - claim,
Pleased as Man with man to dwell,

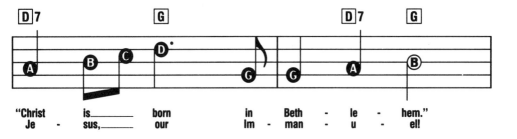

"Christ is_____ born in Beth - le - hem."
Je - sus,_____ our Im - man - u - el!

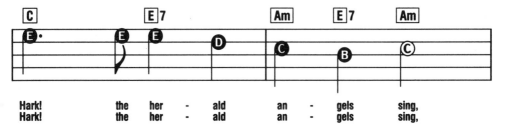

Hark! the her - ald an - gels sing,
Hark! the her - ald an - gels sing,

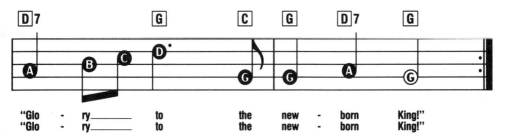

"Glo - ry_____ to the new - born King!"
"Glo - ry_____ to the new - born King!"

Here We Come A-Wassailing

Regi-Sound Program: 3
Rhythm: 6/8 March or Waltz

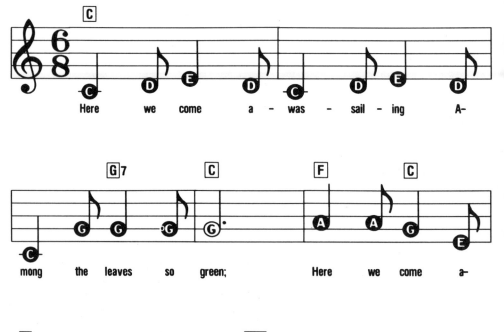

Here we come a – was – sail – ing A-
mong the leaves so green; Here we come a-

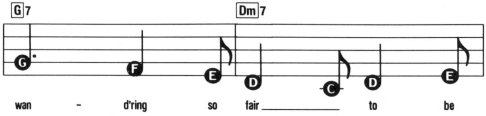

wan – d'ring so fair _____ to be

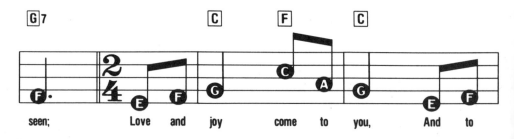

seen; Love and joy come to you, And to

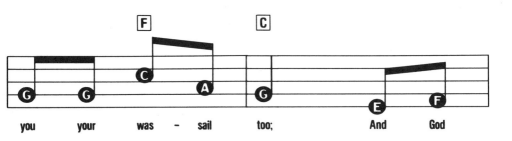

you your was - sail too; And God

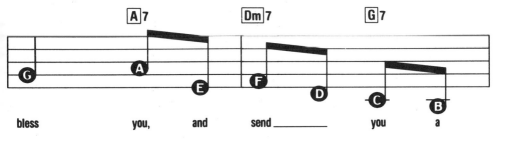

bless you, and send _____ you a

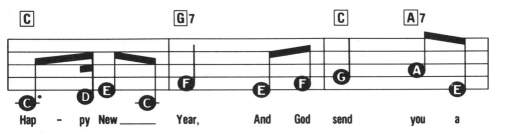

Hap - py New _____ Year, And God send you a

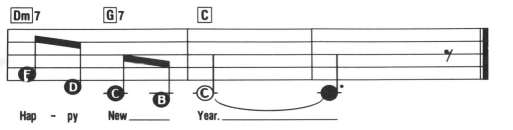

Hap - py New _____ Year. _____

The Holly And The Ivy

Regi-Sound Program: 1
Rhythm: Waltz

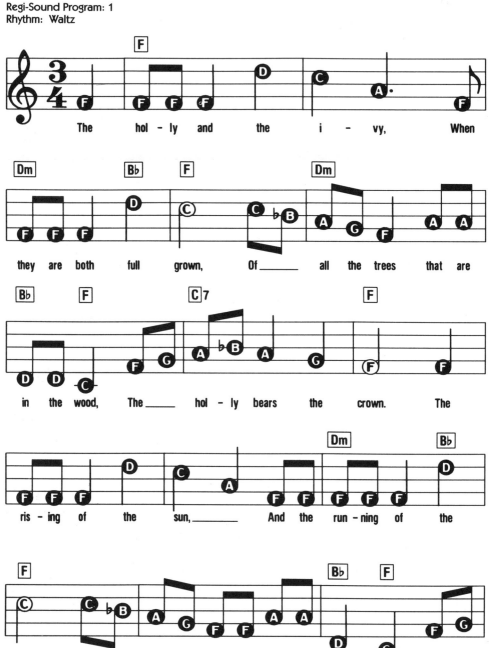

83

A Holly Jolly Christmas

Regi-Sound Program: 9
Rhythm: Fox Trot or Swing

Words and Music by
Johnny Marks

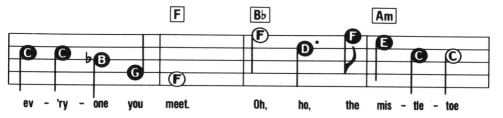

ev - 'ry - one you meet. Oh, ho, the mis - tle - toe

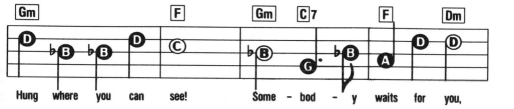

Hung where you can see! Some - bod - y waits for you,

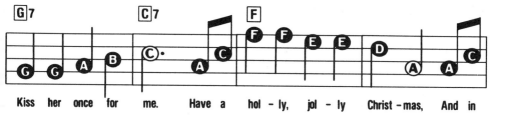

Kiss her once for me. Have a hol - ly, jol - ly Christ - mas, And in

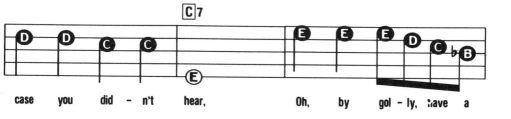

case you did - n't hear, Oh, by gol - ly, have a

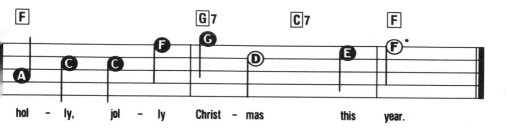

hol - ly, jol - ly Christ - mas this year.

(There's No Place Like)
Home For The Holidays

Regi-Sound Program: 5
Rhythm: Fox Trot or Swing

Words by Al Stillman
Music by Robert Allen

Here Comes Santa Claus
(Right Down Santa Claus Lane)

Words and Music by Gene Autry
and Oakley Haldeman

Regi-Sound Program: 4
Rhythm: Swing

Here comes San - ta Claus! Here comes San - ta Claus! Right down San - ta Claus

Lane!
1. Vix - en and Blitz - en and all his rein - deer are
2. He's got a bag that is filled with toys for the

pull - ing on the rein. Bells are ring - ing,
boys and girls a - gain. Hear those sleigh - bells

chil - dren sing - ing, all is mer - ry and bright.
jin - gle jan - gle, what a beau - ti - ful sight.

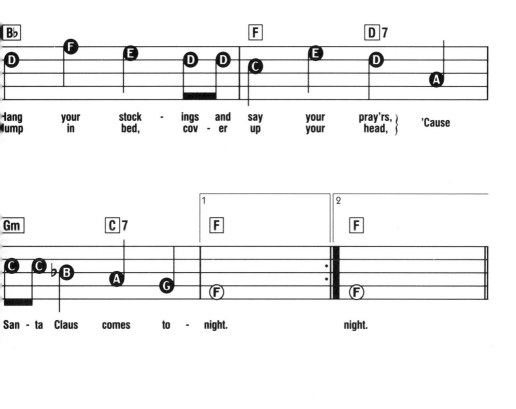

Hang your stock - ings and say your pray'rs, ⎫
Jump in bed, cov - er up your head, ⎭ 'Cause

San - ta Claus comes to - night. night.

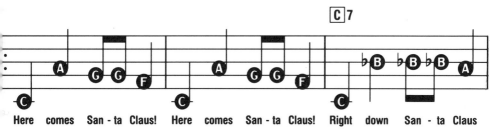

Here comes San - ta Claus! Here comes San - ta Claus! Right down San - ta Claus

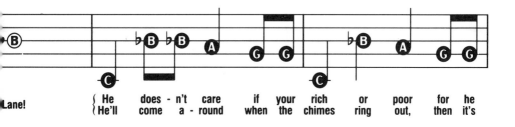

Lane! ⎰ He does - n't care if your rich or poor for he
      ⎱ He'll come a - round when the chimes ring out, then it's

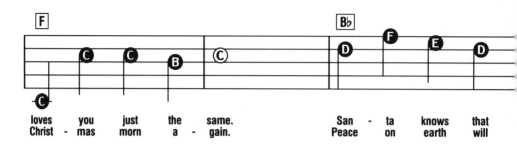

loves you just the same. / Christ - mas morn a - gain. San - ta knows that / Peace on earth will

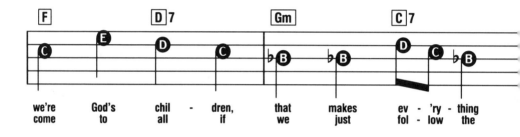

we're God's chil - dren, that makes ev - 'ry - thing / come to all if we just fol - low the

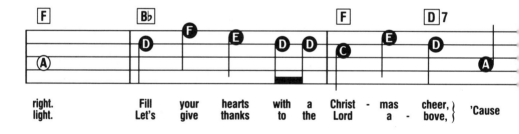

right. Fill your hearts with a Christ - mas cheer, } 'Cause / light. Let's give thanks to the Lord a - bove,

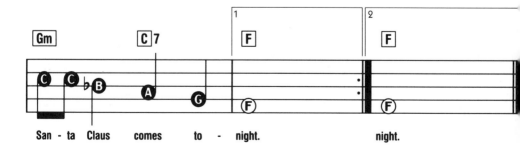

San - ta Claus comes to - night. night.

It's Just Another New Year's Eve

Regi-Sound Program: 2
Rhythm: Swing

Music by Barry Manilow
Lyric by Marty Panzer

1. Don't look so sad. _____ It's not so
_____ But we've made
3. *(See additional lyrics)*

bad, you know. It's just an - oth - er night, that's all it
good friend, too. Re - mem - ber all the nights we've spent with

is. It's not the first. It's not the worst you know. We've come through
them and all our plans. Who says they can't come true? _____ To - night's an -

all the rest. We'll get through this. 2. We've made mis - takes _____

oth – er chance   to start a – gain.
it's only New Year's Eve.   It's just an –

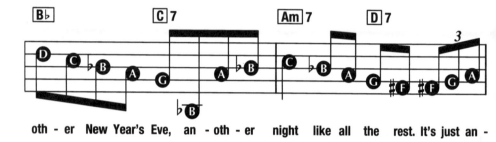

oth – er New Year's Eve, an – oth – er night like all the rest. It's just an –

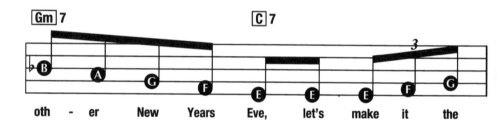

oth – er New Years Eve, let's make it the

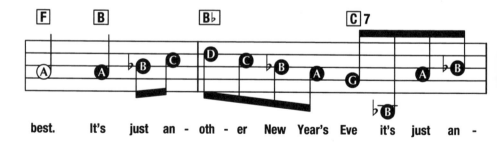

best. It's just an – oth – er New Year's Eve it's just an –

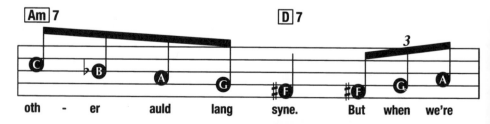

oth – er auld lang syne. But when we're

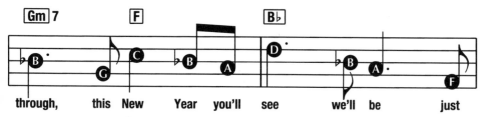

through, this New Year you'll see we'll be just

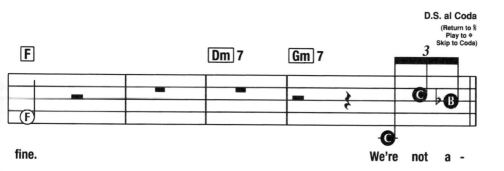

fine.   We're not a -

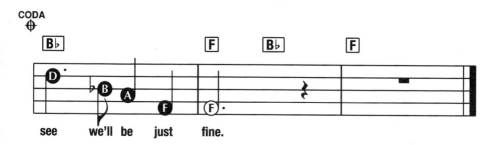

see we'll be just fine.

Additional Lyrics

3. We're not alone,
   We've got the world, you know.
   And it won't let us down,
   Just wait and see.
   And we'll grow old,
   But think how wise we'll grow,
   There's more you know,
   It's only New Year's Eve.

   (*Chorus*)

I Heard The Bells On Christmas Day

Words by Henry Longfellow
Adapted by Johnny Marks
Music by Johnny Marks

Regi-Sound Program: 6
Rhythm: Pops or 8 Beat

95

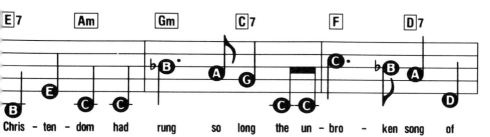

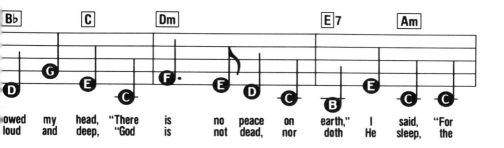

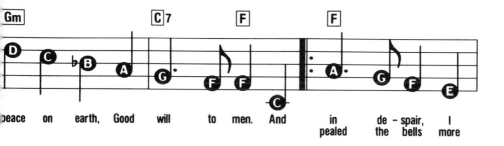

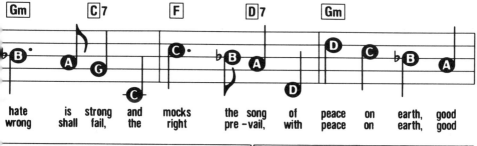

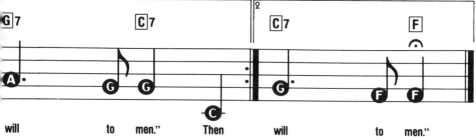

I Heard The Bells On Christmas Day

Regi-Sound Program: 9
Rhythm: Pops or 8 Beat

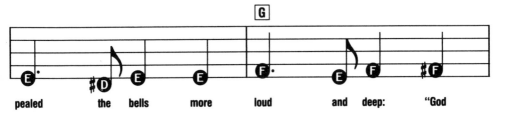

pealed   the   bells   more   loud   and   deep: "God

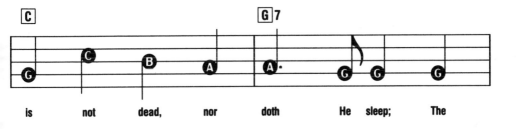

is   not   dead,   nor   doth   He   sleep;   The

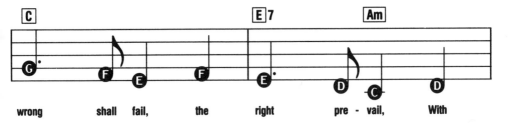

wrong   shall   fail,   the   right   pre - vail,   With

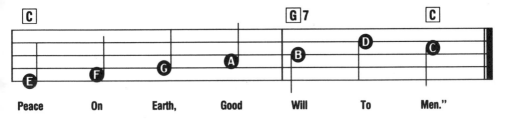

Peace   On   Earth,   Good   Will   To   Men."

I Saw Mommy Kissing Santa Claus

Regi-Sound Program: 5
Rhythm: Fox Trot or Swing

Words and Music by
Tommie Connor

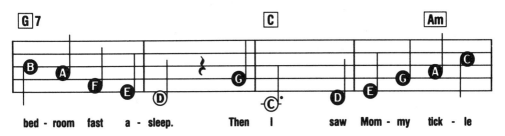

bed - room fast a - sleep. Then I saw Mom - my tick - le

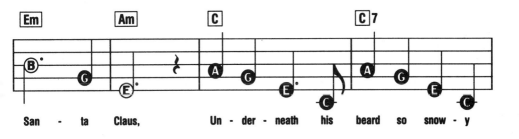

San - ta Claus, Un - der - neath his beard so snow - y

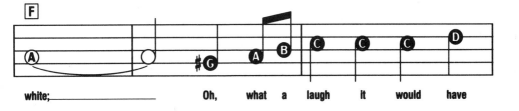

white;_____ Oh, what a laugh it would have

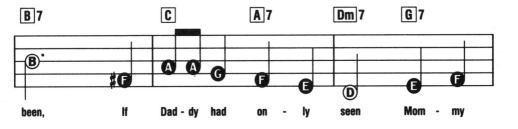

been, If Dad - dy had on - ly seen Mom - my

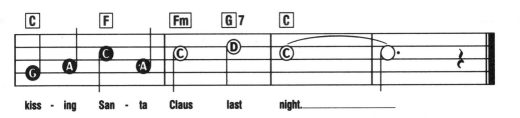

kiss - ing San - ta Claus last night._____

I Saw Three Ships

Regi-Sound Program: 2
Rhythm: 6/8 March or Waltz

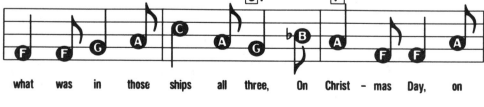

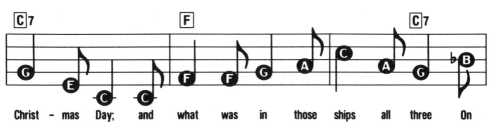

Christ - mas Day; and what was in those ships all three On

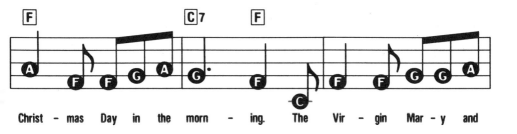

Christ - mas Day in the morn - ing. The Vir - gin Mar - y and

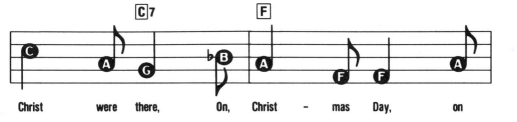

Christ were there, On, Christ - mas Day, on

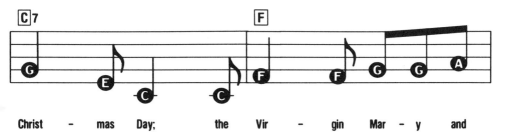

Christ - mas Day; the Vir - gin Mar - y and

Christ were there, On Christ - mas Day in the morn - ing.

I'll Be Home For Christmas

Regi-Sound Program: 1
Rhythm: Fox Trot or Swing

Words and Music by Kim Gannon
and Walter Kent

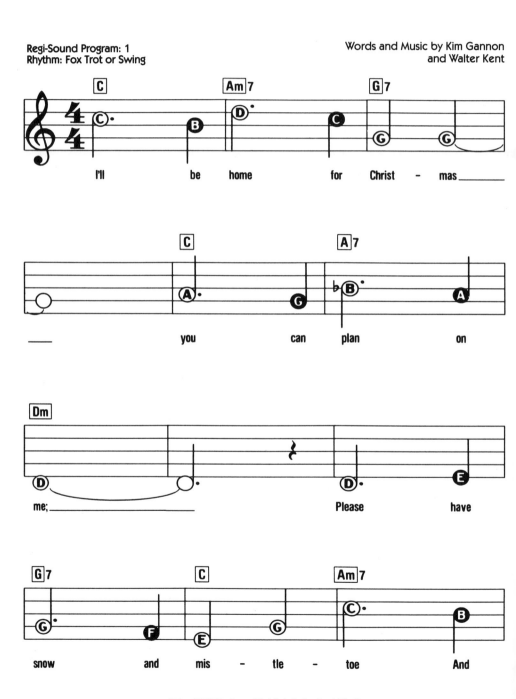

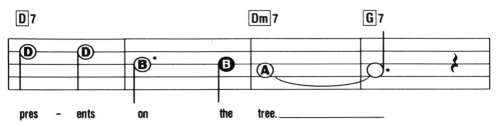

pres - ents on the tree. _____

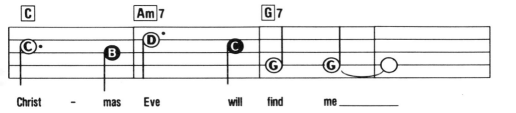

Christ - mas Eve will find me _____

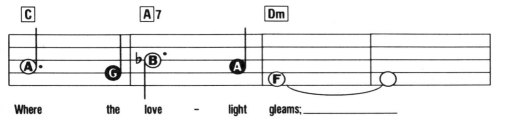

Where the love - light gleams; _____

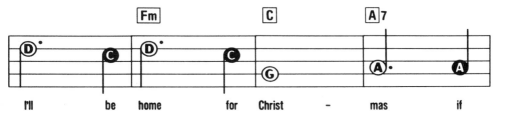

I'll be home for Christ - mas if

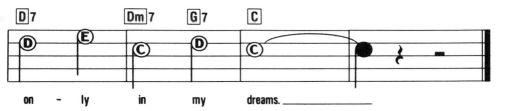

on - ly in my dreams. _____

It Came Upon The Midnight Clear

Regi-Sound Program: 1
Rhythm: Waltz

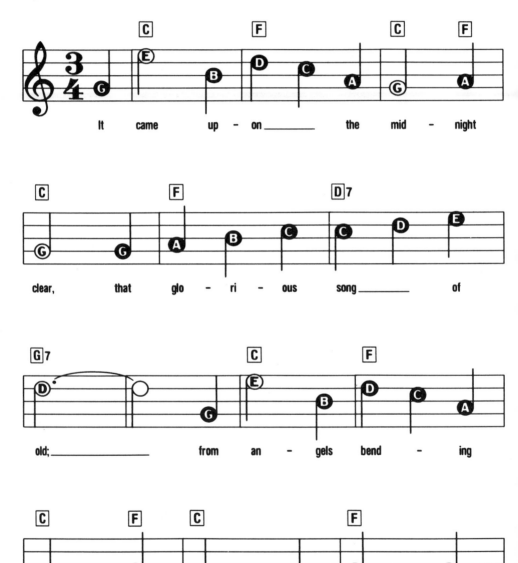

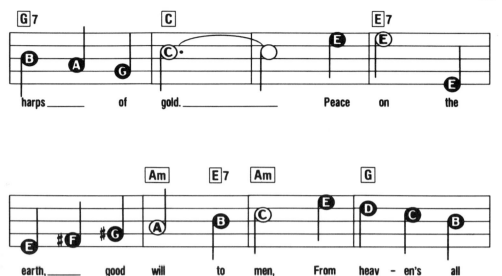

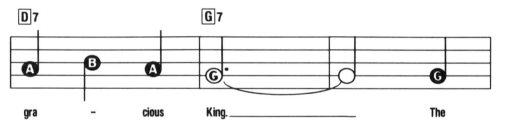

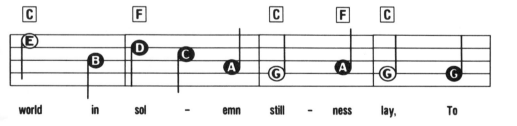

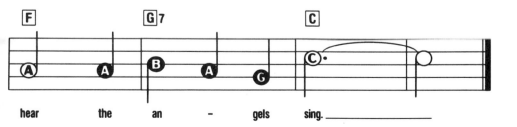

It's Christmas All Over The World

Regi-Sound Program: 5
Rhythm: Fox Trot or Swing

Words and Music by Bill House
and John Hobe

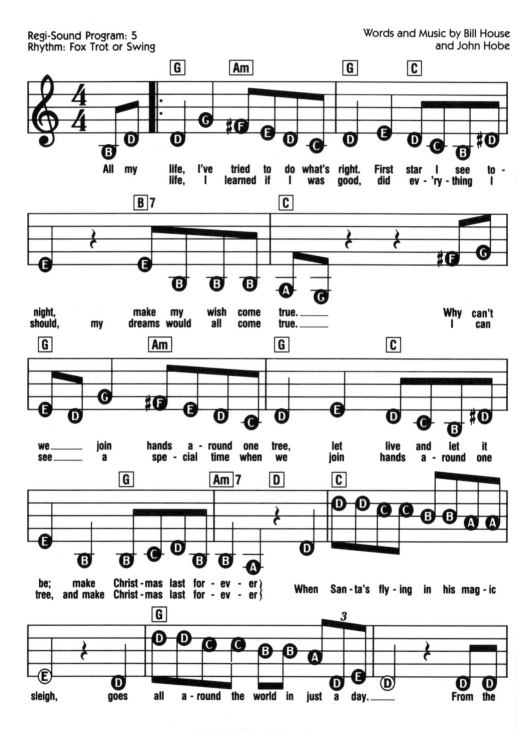

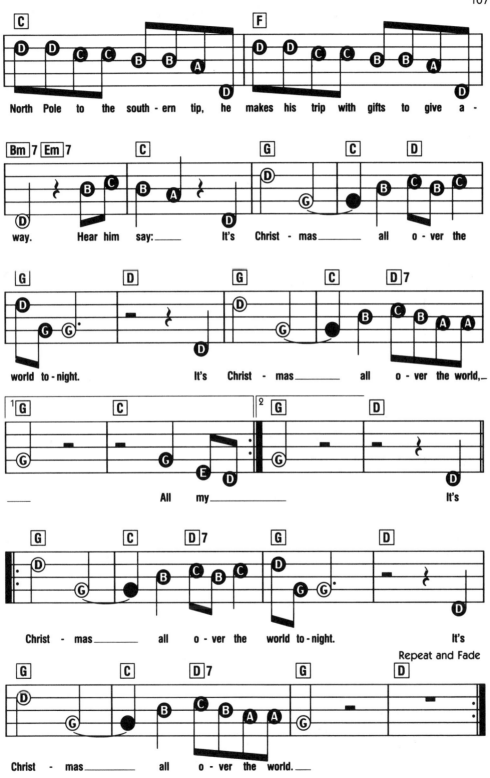

Jingle-Bell Rock

Regi-Sound Program: 5
Rhythm: Rock or Fox Trot

Words and Music by Joe Beal
and Jim Boothe

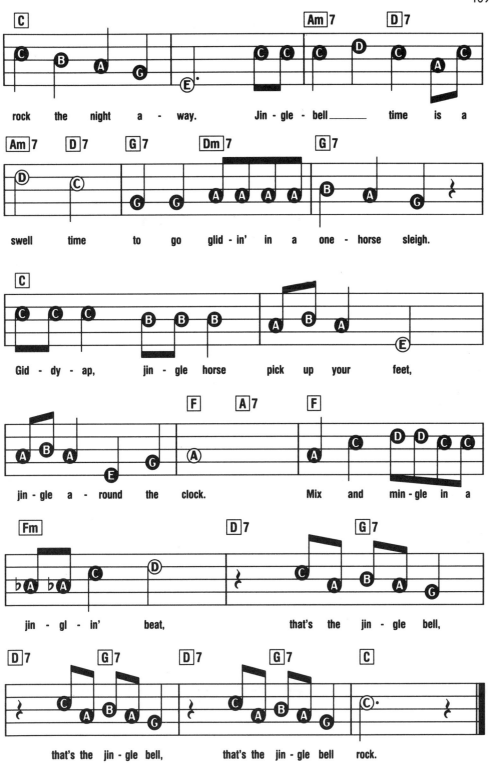

Jingle Bells

Regi-Sound Program: 5
Rhythm: Fox Trot or Polka

Dash - ing through the snow, in a one - horse o - pen

sleigh; O'er the fields we go, laugh - ing all the

way, Bells on bob - tail ring, mak - ing spir - its

bright; what fun it is to ride and sing a

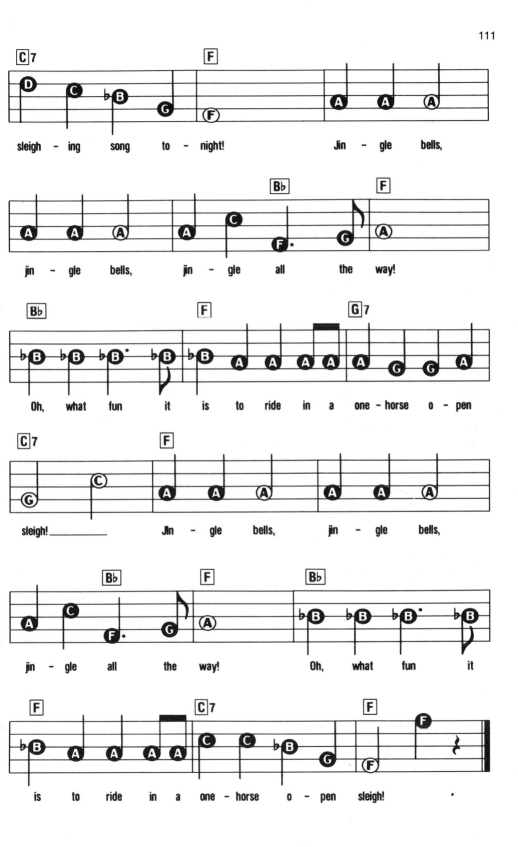

Jolly Old St. Nicholas

Regi-Sound Program: 2
Rhythm: Fox Trot or Swing

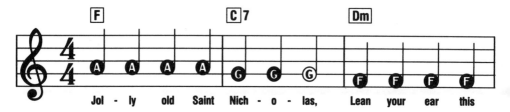

Jol - ly old Saint Nich - o - las, Lean your ear this

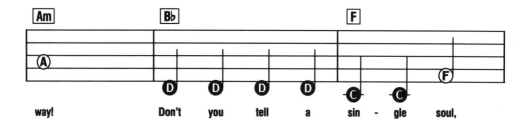

way! Don't you tell a sin - gle soul,

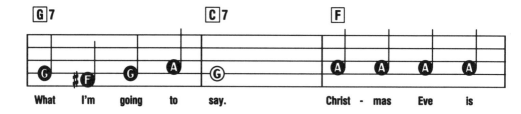

What I'm going to say. Christ - mas Eve is

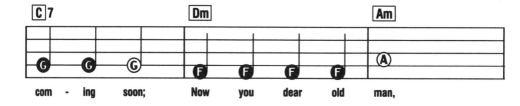

com - ing soon; Now you dear old man,

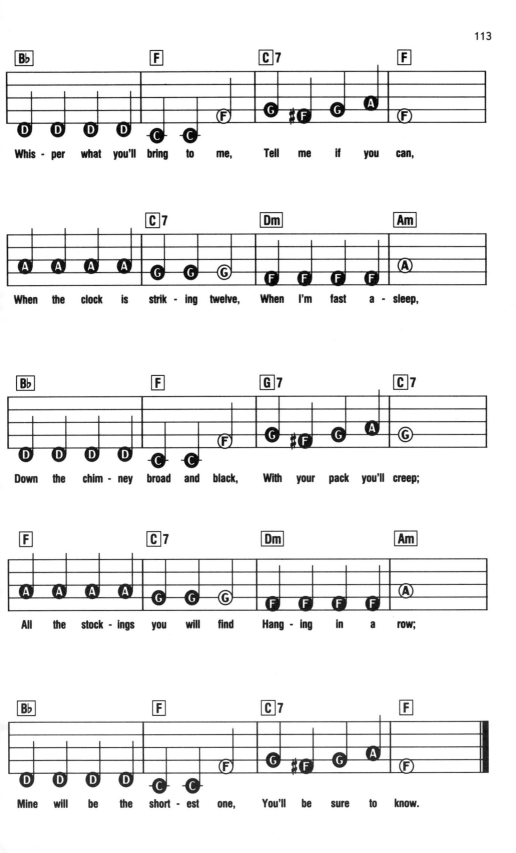

Joy To The World

Regi-Sound Program: 9
Rhythm: March

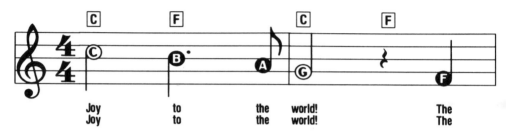

Joy to the world! The
Joy to the world! The

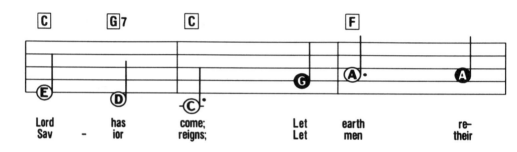

Lord has come; Let earth re-
Sav - ior reigns; Let men their

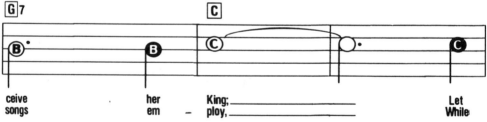

ceive her King;_____ Let
songs em - ploy,_____ While

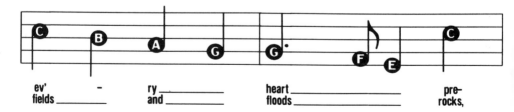

ev' - ry_____ heart_____ pre-
fields_____ and_____ floods_____ rocks,

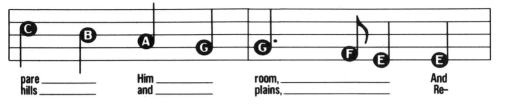

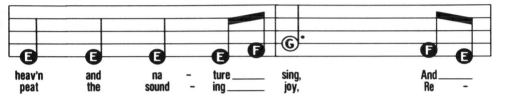

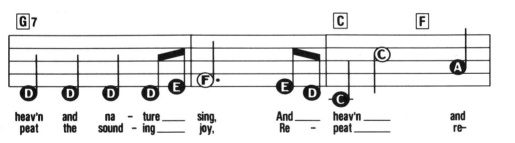

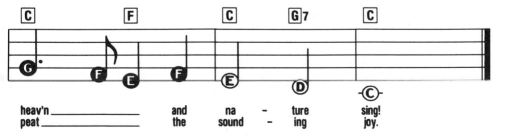

Last Christmas

Regi-Sound Program: 1
Rhythm: Disco or 16 Beat

Words and Music by
George Michae[l]

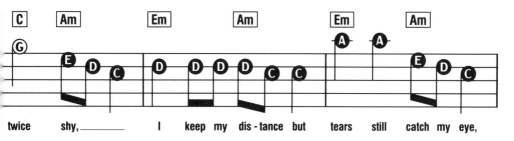

twice shy, _____ I keep my dis - tance but tears still catch my eye,

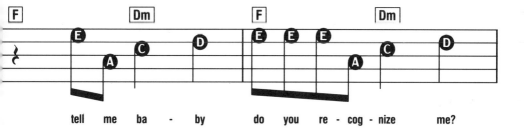

tell me ba - by do you re - cog - nize me?

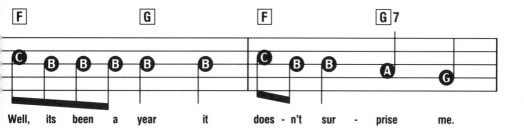

Well, its been a year it does - n't sur - prise me.

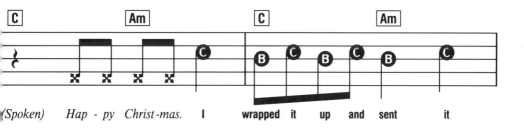

(Spoken) Hap - py Christ -mas. I wrapped it up and sent it

Additional Lyrics

2. A crowded room, friends with tired eyes.
I'm hiding from you and your soul of ice.
My God, I thought you were someone to rely on.
Me, I guess I was a shoulder to cry on.
A face on a lover with a fire in his heart,
A man under cover but you tore me apart.
Oo, now I've found a new love.
You'll never fool me again.

The Last Month Of The Year
(What Month Was Jesus Born In?)

Regi-Sound Program: 10
Rhythm: Pops or Country

Words and Music by Vera Hall
Adapted and Arranged by Ruby Pickens Tartt
and Alan Lomax

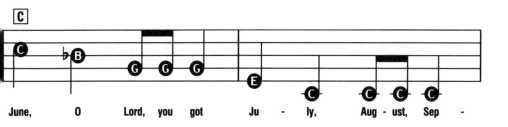

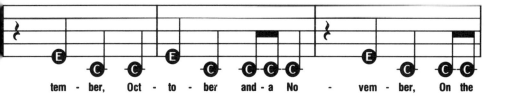

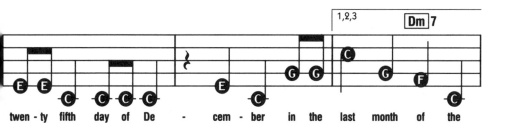

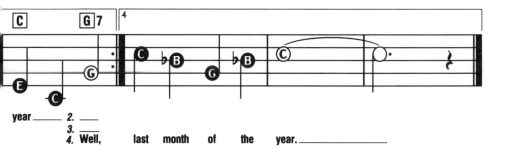

Let It Snow! Let It Snow! Let It Snow!

Regi-Sound Program: 2
Rhythm: Swing or Jazz

Words by Sammy Cahn
Music by Jule Styne

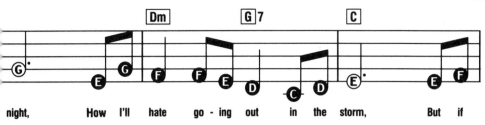

night, How I'll hate go - ing out in the storm, But if

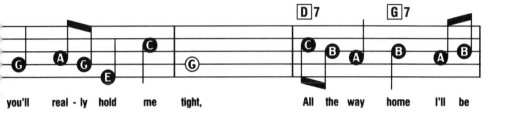

you'll real - ly hold me tight, All the way home I'll be

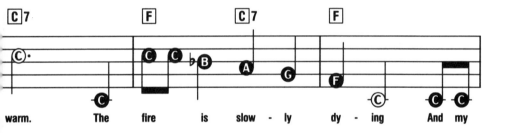

warm. The fire is slow - ly dy - ing And my

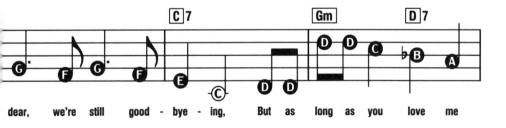

dear, we're still good - bye - ing, But as long as you love me

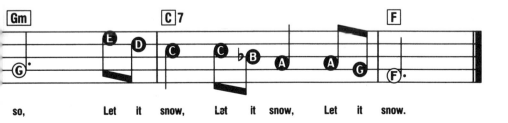

so, Let it snow, Let it snow, Let it snow.

The Little Drummer Boy

Regi-Sound Program: 2
Rhythm: March

Words and Music by Katherine Davis,
Henry Onorati and Harry Simeone

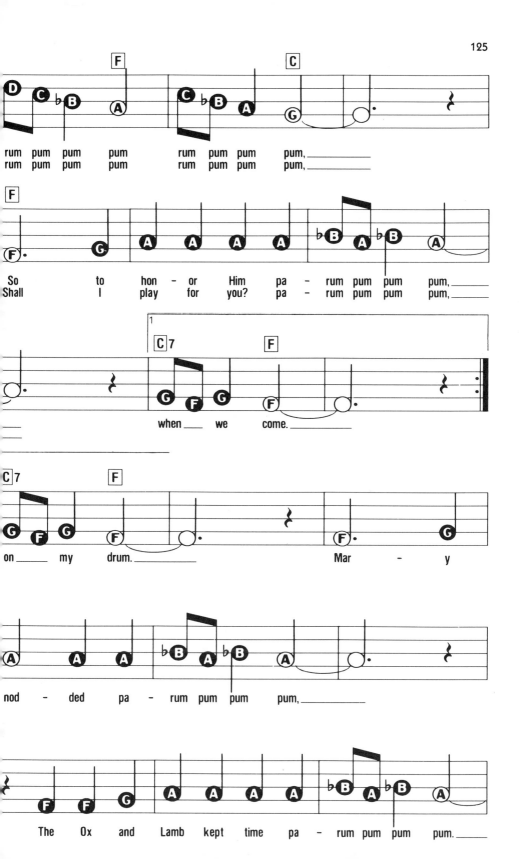

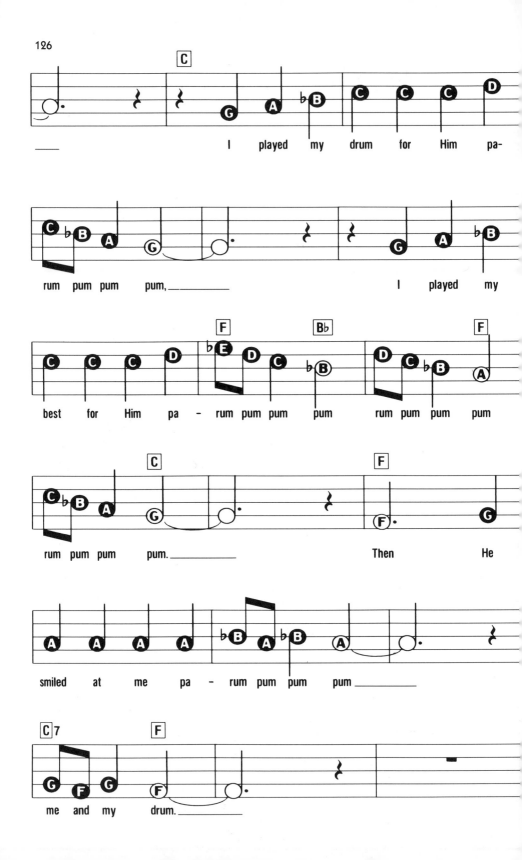

March Of The Toys

Regi-Sound Program: 5
Rhythm: 6/8 March or Waltz

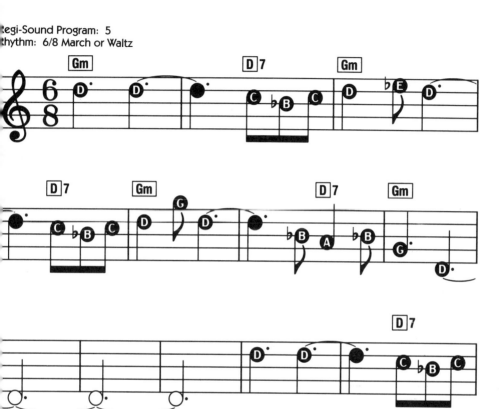

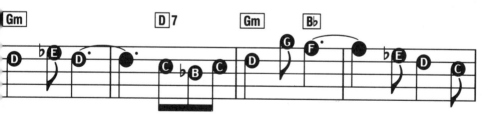

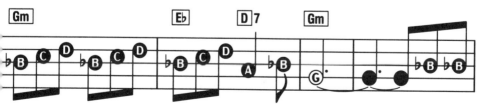

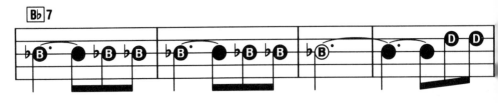

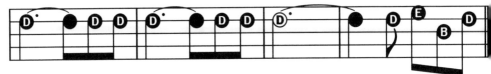

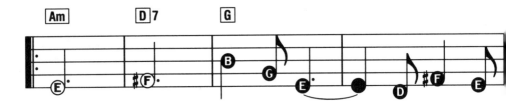

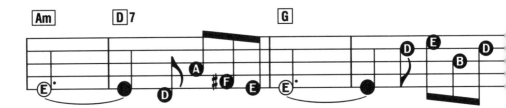

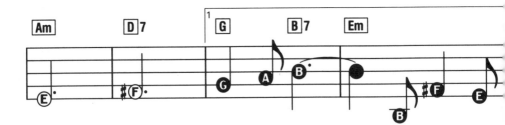

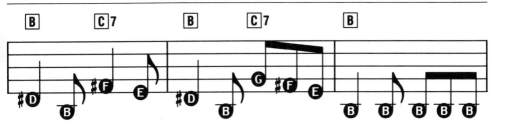

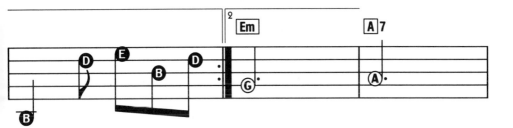

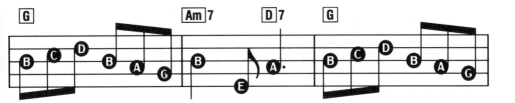

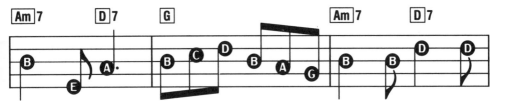

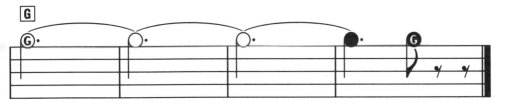

A Marshmallow World

Regi-Sound Program: 2
Rhythm: Fox Trot or Polka

Words by Carl Sigman
Music by Peter De Rose

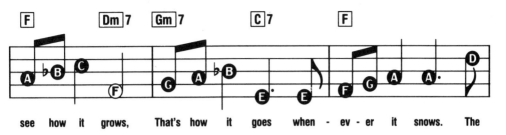

see how it grows, That's how it goes when - ev - er it snows. The

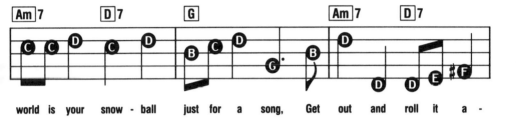

world is your snow - ball just for a song, Get out and roll it a -

long. It's a yum yum - my world made for sweet - hearts, Take a

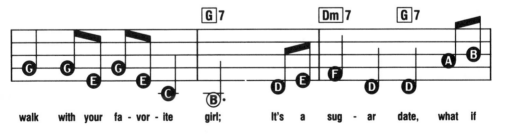

walk with your fa - vor - ite girl; It's a sug - ar date, what if

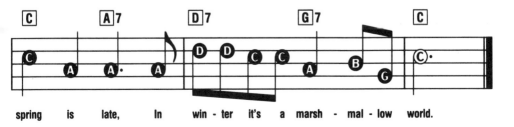

spring is late, In win - ter it's a marsh - mal - low world.

Mele Kalikimaka

Regi-Sound Program: 5
Rhythm: Fox Trot or Swing

Words and Music by
Alex Anderson

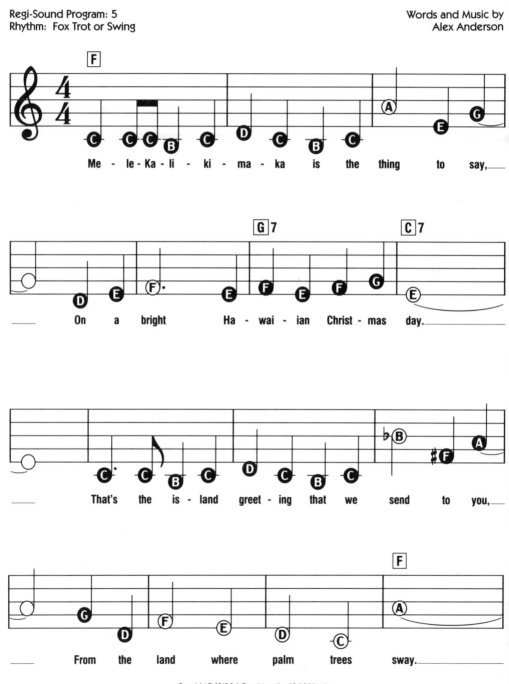

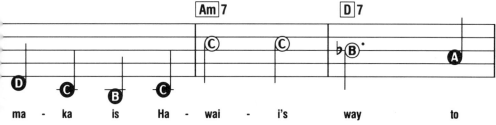

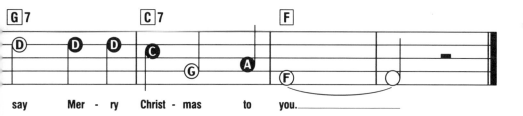

Mistletoe And Holly

Regi-Sound Program: 2
Rhythm: Swing

Words and Music by Frank Sinatra,
Dok Stanford and Henry Sanicola

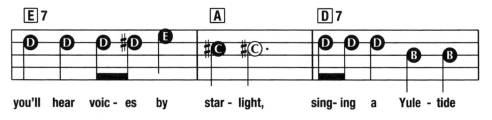

you'll hear voic- es   by   star - light,   sing- ing   a   Yule - tide

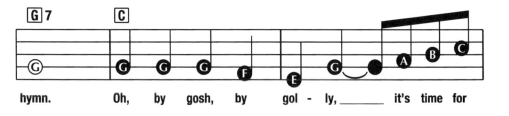

hymn.   Oh,   by   gosh,   by   gol - ly, _____   it's time for

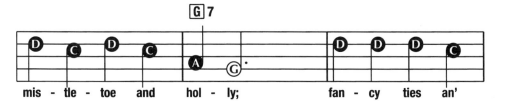

mis - tle - toe   and   hol - ly;   fan - cy   ties   an'

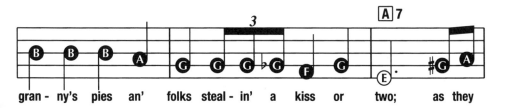

gran- ny's pies an'   folks steal- in' a   kiss or   two;   as they

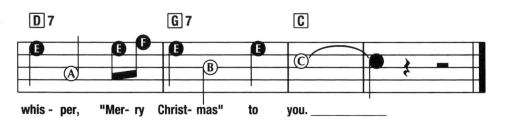

whis - per,   "Mer- ry Christ- mas"   to   you. _____

My Favorite Things
(From "The Sound Of Music")

Regi-Sound Program: 9
Rhythm: Waltz

Lyrics by Oscar Hammerstein II
Music by Richard Rodgers

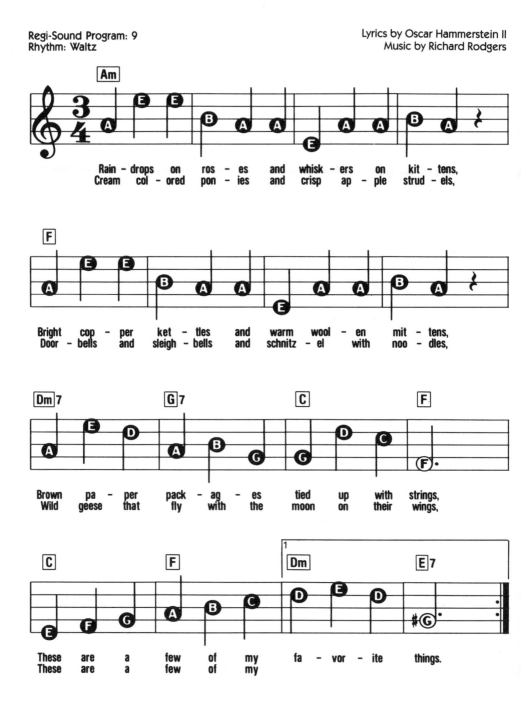

Rain - drops on ros - es and whisk - ers on kit - tens,
Cream col - ored pon - ies and crisp ap - ple strud - els,

Bright cop - per ket - tles and warm wool - en mit - tens,
Door - bells and sleigh - bells and schnitz - el with noo - dles,

Brown pa - per pack - ag - es tied up with strings,
Wild geese that fly with the moon on their wings,

These are a few of my fa - vor - ite things.
These are a few of my

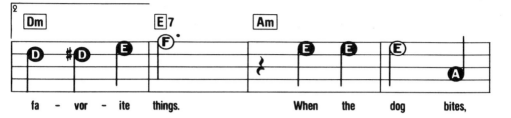

fa - vor - ite things. When the dog bites,

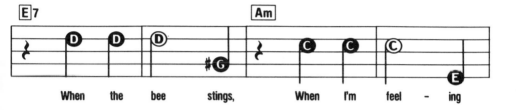

When the bee stings, When I'm feel - ing

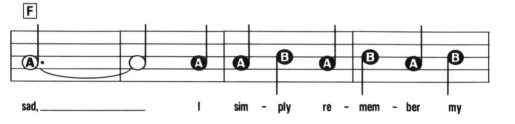

sad,_____ I sim - ply re - mem - ber my

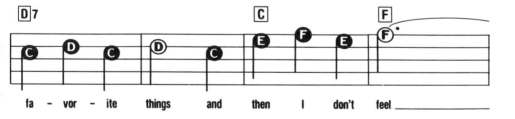

fa - vor - ite things and then I don't feel _____

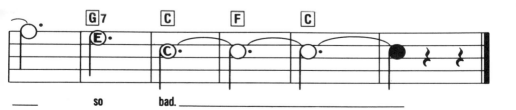

_____ so bad. _____

The Most Wonderful Day Of The Year

Regi-Sound Program: 3
Rhythm: Waltz

Music and Lyrics by
Johnny Marks

1 A 3 pack - ful of toys means a sack - ful of joys for
2 Jack in the box waits for chil - dren to shout, "Wake
4 won't seem like Christ - mas till Dad gets his tie, " It's

mil - lions of girls and for mil - lions of boys }
up, don't you know that it's time to ccme out!" } When
just what I want - ed," is his year - ly cry!

Christ - mas Day is here _____ The most

won - der - ful day of the year! _____ 2. A
4. It

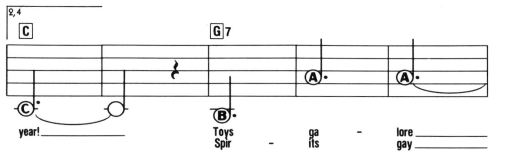

year! _____ Toys ga - lore _____
Spir - its gay _____

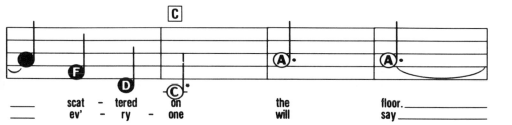

—— scat - tered on the floor.
—— ev' - ry - one will say _____

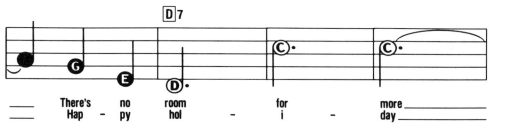

—— There's no room for more _____
—— Hap - py hol - i - day _____

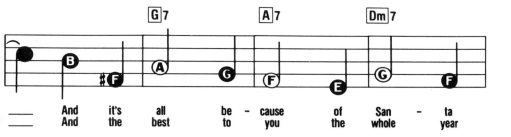

—— And it's all be - cause of San - ta
And the best to you the whole year

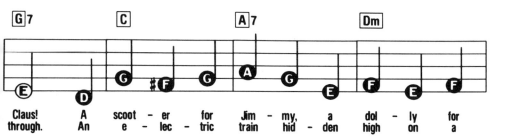

Claus! A scoot - er for Jim - my, a dol - ly for
through. An e - lec - tric train hid - den high on a

140

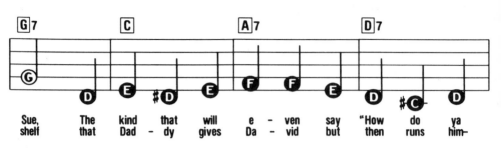

Sue, The kind that will e – ven say "How do ya
shelf that Dad – dy gives Da – vid but then runs him –

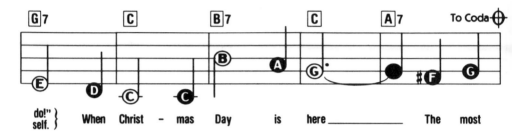

do!" ⎫
self. ⎬ When Christ – mas Day is here _____ The most

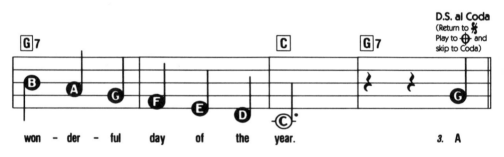

won – der – ful day of the year. 3. A

CODA

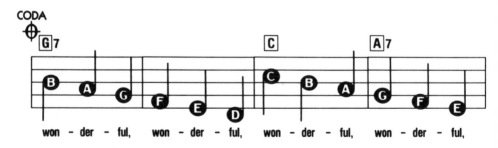

won – der – ful, won – der – ful, won – der – ful, won – der – ful,

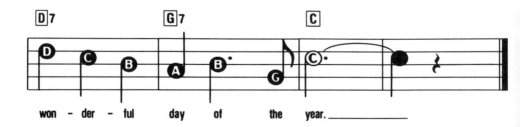

won – der – ful day of the year. _____

The Night Before Christmas Song

Music by Johnny Marks
Lyrics adapted by Johnny Marks
from Clement Moore's poem

Regi-Sound Program: 3
Rhythm: Waltz

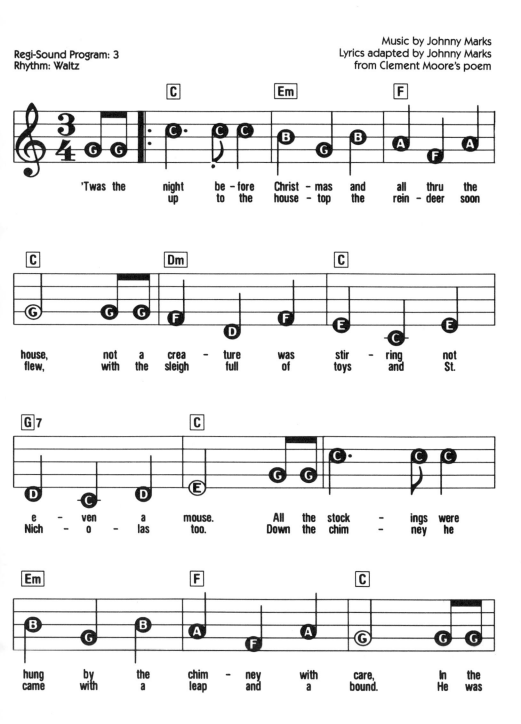

142

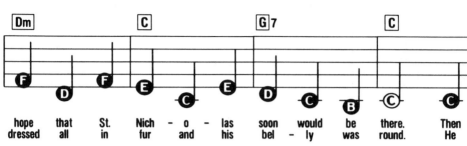

hope that St. Nich – o – las soon would be there. Then
dressed all in fur and his bel – ly was round. He

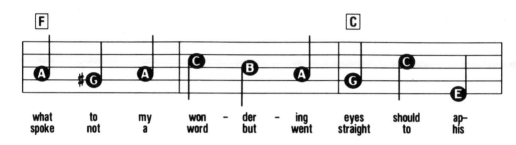

what to my won – der – ing eyes should ap-
spoke not a word but went straight to his

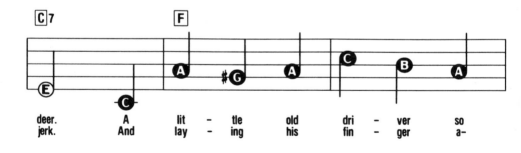

pear, A min – ia – ture sleigh and eight ti – ny rein-
work And filled all the stock – ings, then turned with a

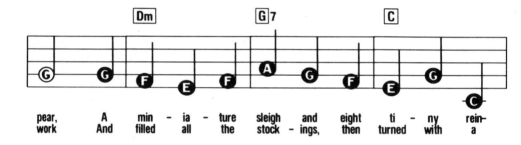

deer. A lit – tle old dri – ver so
jerk. And lay – ing his fin – ger a-

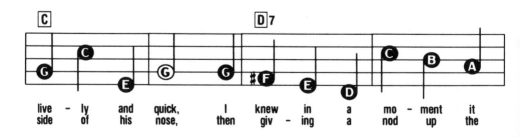

live – ly and quick, I knew in a mo – ment it
side of his nose, then giv – ing a nod up the

143

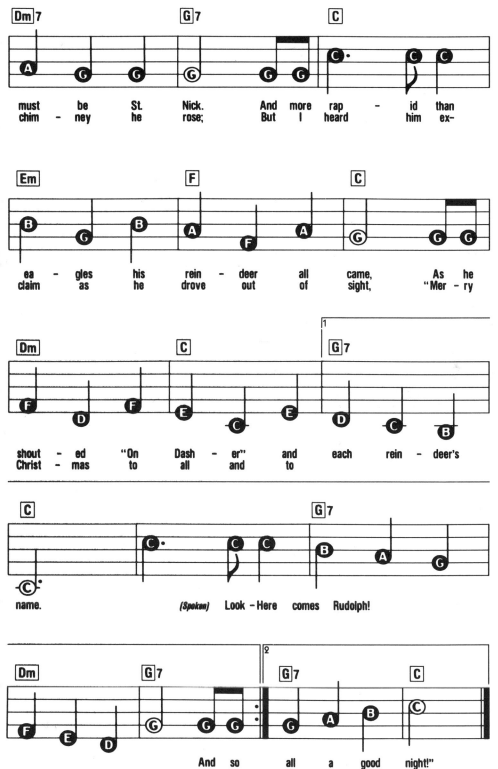

Nuttin' For Christmas

Regi-Sound Program: 2
Rhythm: Fox Trot or Shuffle

Words and Music by Roy Bennett
and Sid Tepper

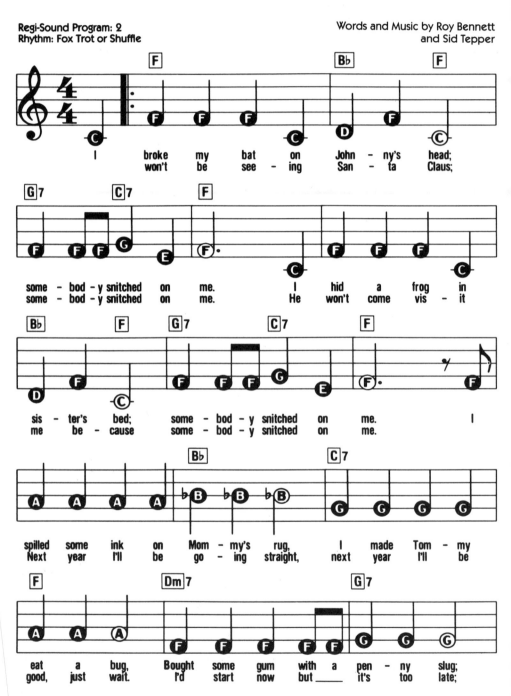

O Christmas Tree

Regi-Sound Program: 3
Rhythm: Waltz

O Come All Ye Faithful

Regi-Sound Program: 6
Rhythm: March or None

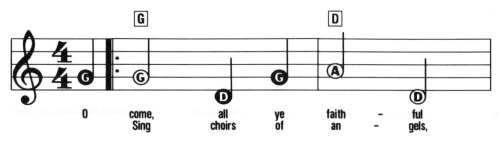

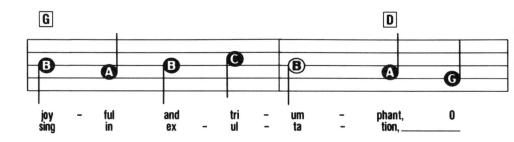

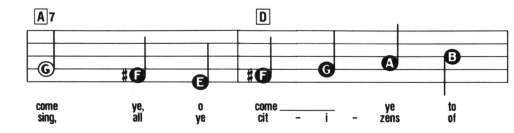

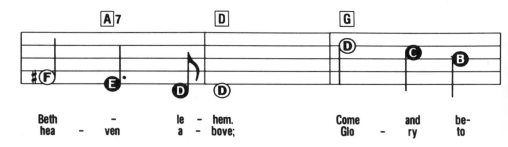

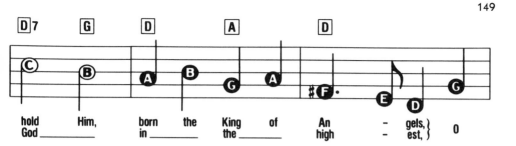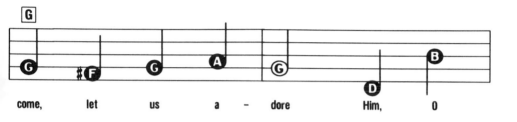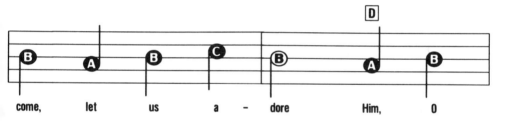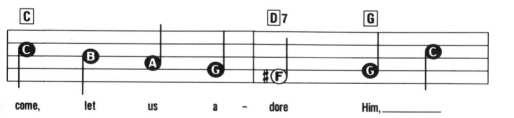

O Holy Night

Regi-Sound Program: 6
Rhythm: None

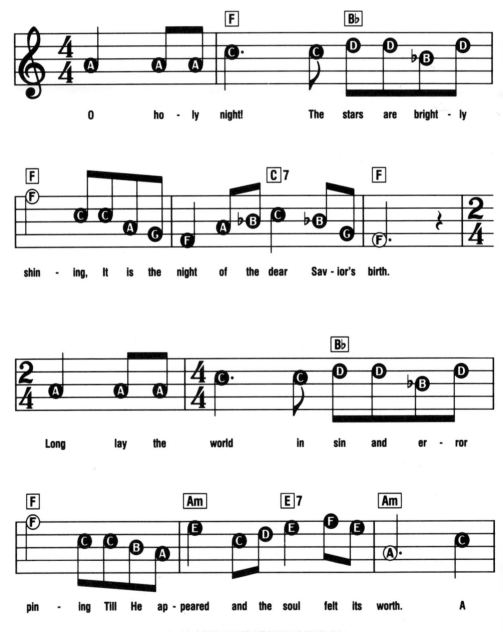

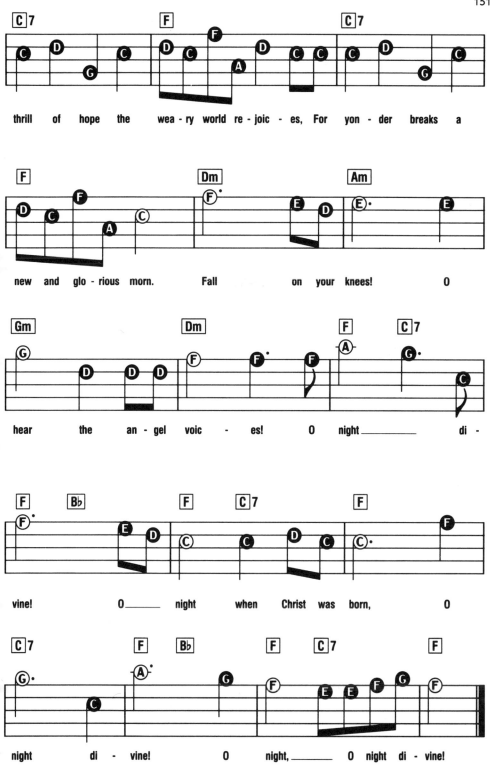

O Little Town Of Bethlehem

Regi-Sound Program: 1
Rhythm: Pops or Fox Trot

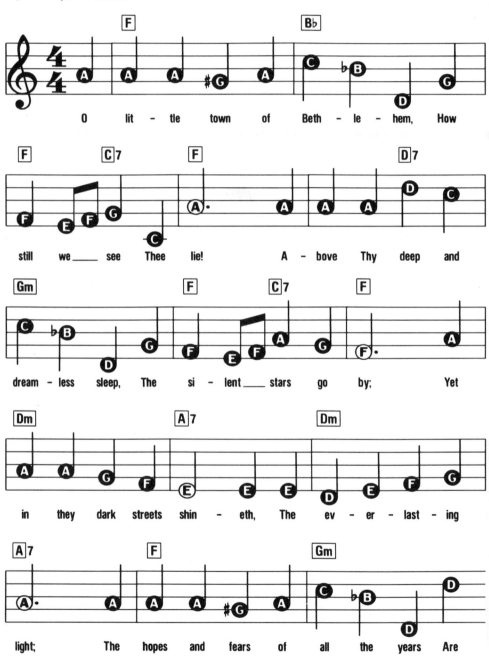

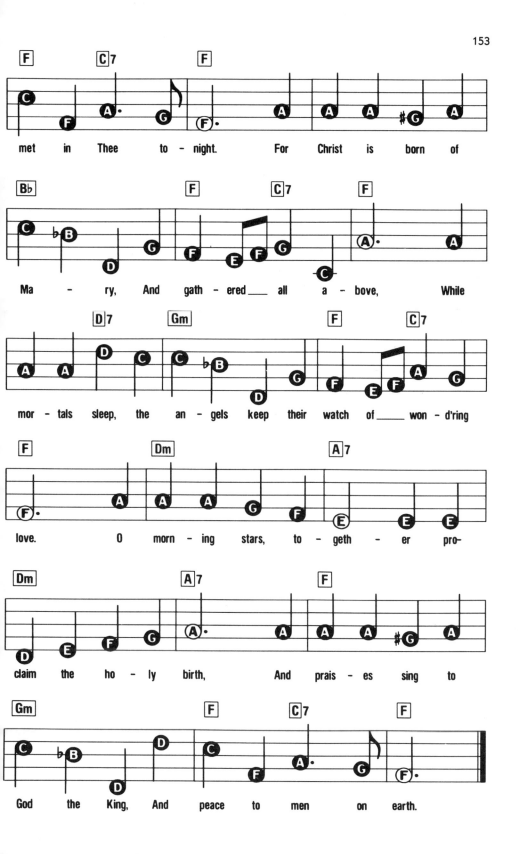

Parade Of The Wooden Soldiers

Regi-Sound Program: 5
Rhythm: March or Polka

By Ballard MacDonald
and Leon Jessel

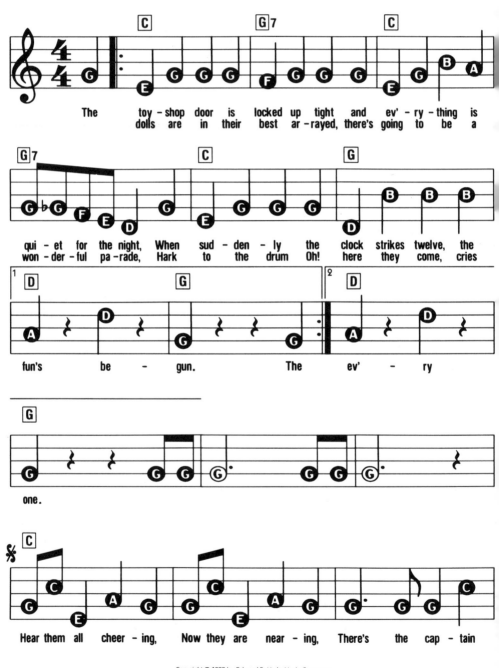

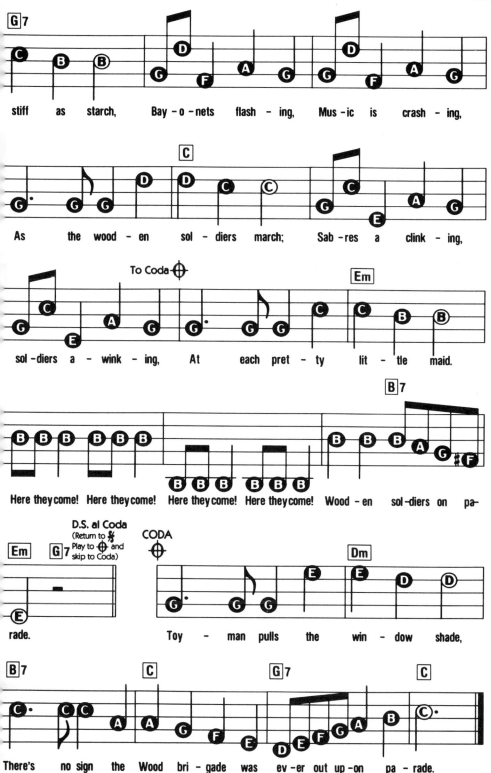

Pretty Paper

Regi-Sound Program: 3
Rhythm: Waltz

Words and Music by
Willie Nelson

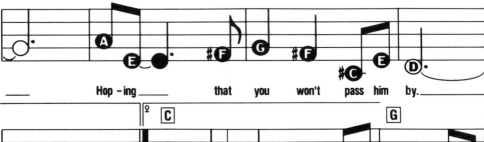

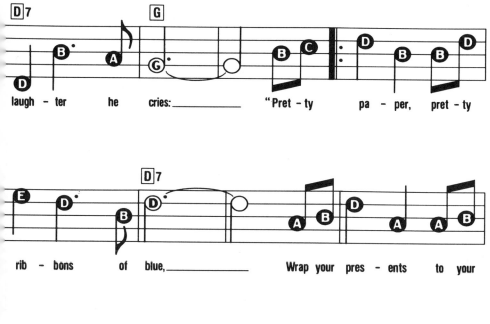

laugh - ter he cries:_____ "Pret - ty pa - per, pret - ty

rib - bons of blue,_____ Wrap your pres - ents to your

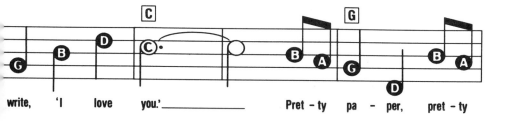

dar - ling from you._____ Pret - ty pen - cils to

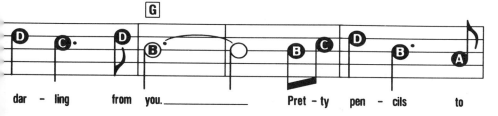

write, 'I love you.'_____ Pret - ty pa - per, pret - ty

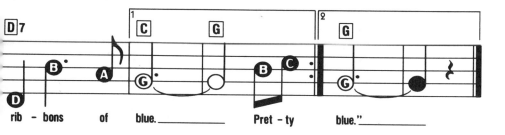

rib - bons of blue._____ Pret - ty blue."_____

Rockin' Around The Christmas Tree

Regi-Sound Program: 7
Rhythm: Fox Trot, Polka or Shuffle

Music and Lyrics by
Johnny Marks

Rudolph The Red-Nosed Reindeer

Regi-Sound Program: 4
Rhythm: Fox Trot or Swing

Music and Lyrics by
Johnny Marks

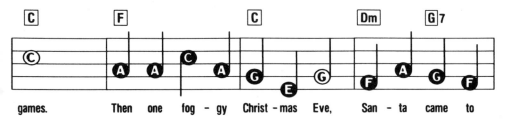

games.   Then   one   fog – gy   Christ-mas   Eve,   San - ta   came   to

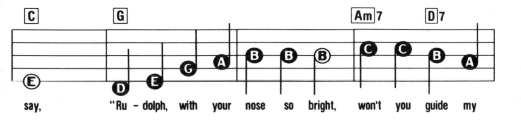

say,   "Ru – dolph, with   your   nose   so   bright,   won't   you   guide   my

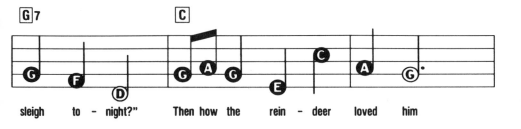

sleigh   to – night?"   Then how   the   rein – deer   loved   him

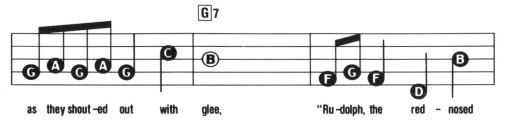

as   they shout –ed   out   with   glee,   "Ru–dolph, the   red – nosed

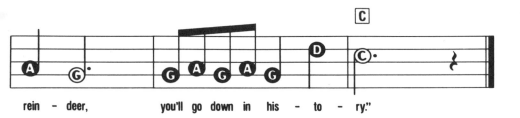

rein - deer,   you'll go down in his – to – ry."

Santa Baby

Regi-Sound Program: 3
Rhythm: Swing

Words and Music by Joan Javits
Phil Springer and Tong Springer

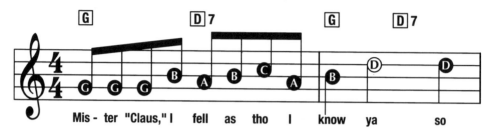

Mis - ter "Claus," I fell as tho I know ya so

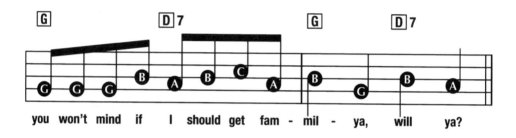

you won't mind if I should get fam - mil - ya, will ya?

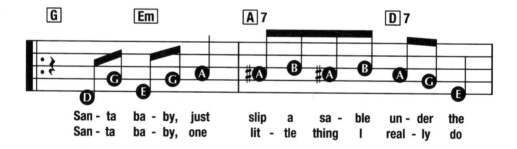

San - ta ba - by, just slip a sa - ble un - der the
San - ta ba - by, one lit - tle thing I real - ly do

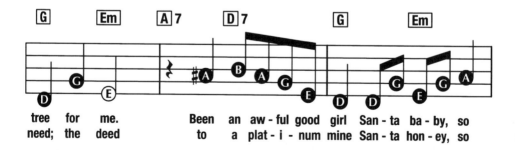

tree for me. Been an aw - ful good girl San - ta ba - by, so
need; the deed to a plat - i - num mine San - ta hon - ey, so

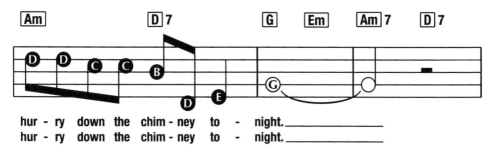

hur - ry down the chim - ney to - night._____

hur - ry down the chim - ney to - night._____

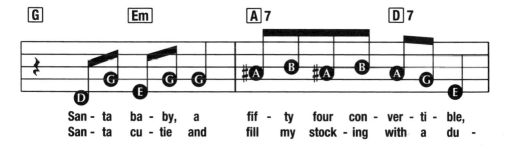

San - ta ba - by, a fif - ty four con - ver - ti - ble,

San - ta cu - tie and fill my stock - ing with a du -

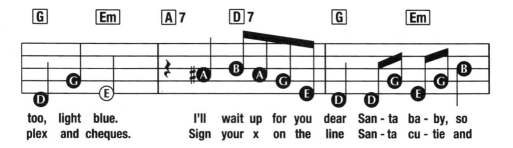

too, light blue. I'll wait up for you dear San - ta ba - by, so

plex and cheques. Sign your x on the line San - ta cu - tie and

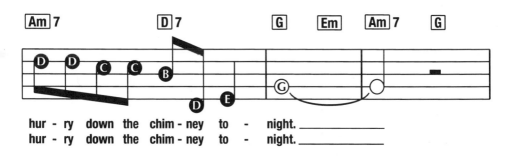

hur - ry down the chim - ney to - night. _____

hur - ry down the chim - ney to - night. _____

B7

Think   of   all   the   fun   I've   missed
Come   and   trim   my   Christ - mas   tree

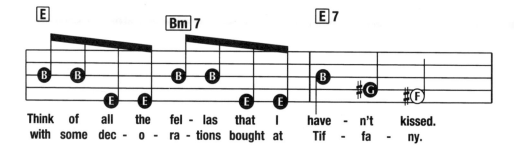

E   Bm 7   E 7

Think   of   all   the   fel - las   that   I   have - n't   kissed.
with   some   dec - o - ra - tions bought at   Tif - fa - ny.

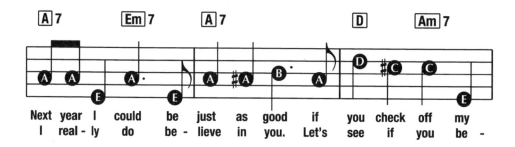

A 7   Em 7   A 7   D   Am 7

Next   year   I   could   be   just   as   good   if   you   check   off   my
I   real - ly   do   be - lieve   in   you. Let's   see   if   you   be -

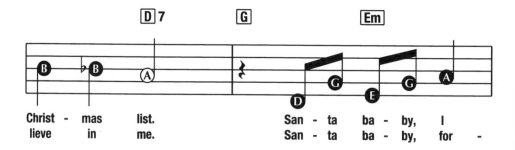

D 7   G   Em

Christ - mas   list.   San - ta   ba - by,   I
lieve   in   me.   San - ta   ba - by,   for -

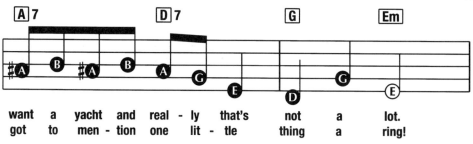

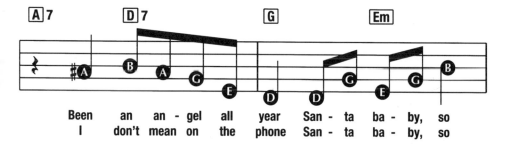

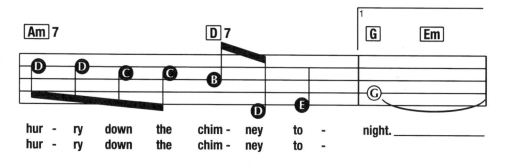

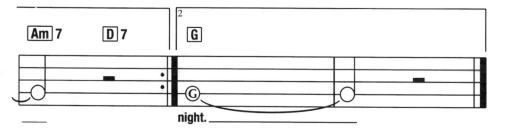

Santa, Bring My Baby Back (To Me)

Regi-Sound Program: 5
Rhythm: March

Words and Music by Claude DeMetrius
and Aaron Schroeder

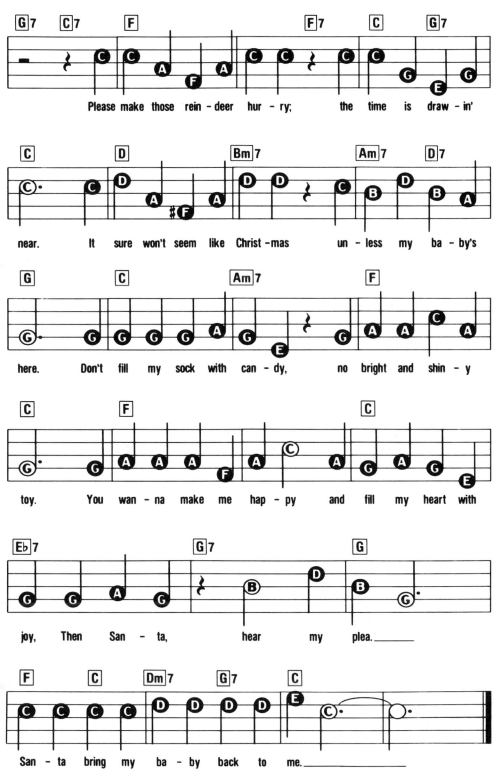

Santa Claus Is Coming To Town

Regi-Sound Program: 3
Rhythm: Swing or Big Band

Words by Haven Gillespie
Music by J. Fred Coots

Silent Night

Regi-Sound Program: 1
Rhythm: Waltz

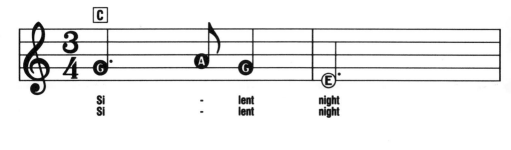

Si - lent night
Si - lent night

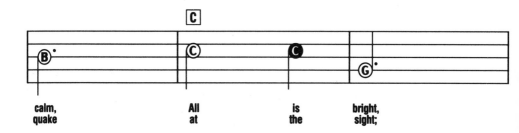

Ho - ly night
Ho - ly night

All is
Shep - herds

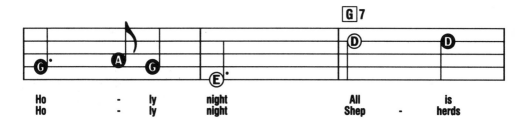

calm,
quake

All
at

is
the

bright,
sight;

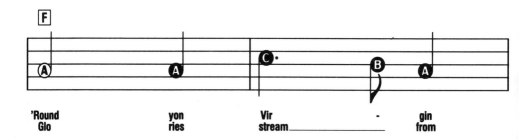

'Round
Glo

yon
ries

Vir
stream _____

gin
from

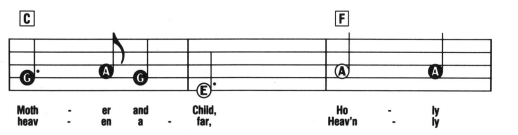

Moth - er and Child, Ho - ly
heav - en a - far, Heav'n - ly

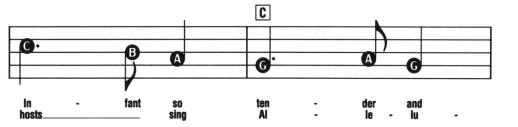

In - fant so ten - der and
hosts_____ sing Al - le - lu -

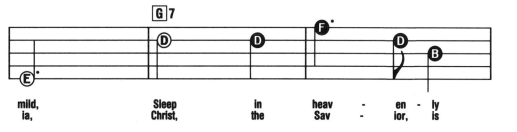

mild, Sleep in heav - en - ly
ia, Christ, the Sav - ior, is

peace,_____ Sleep_____ in
born!_____ Christ,_____ the

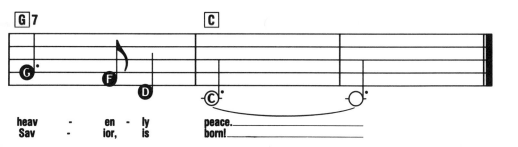

heav - en - ly peace._____
Sav - ior, is born!_____

Silver And Gold

Regi-Sound Program: 2
Rhythm: Waltz

Music and Lyrics by
Johnny Marks

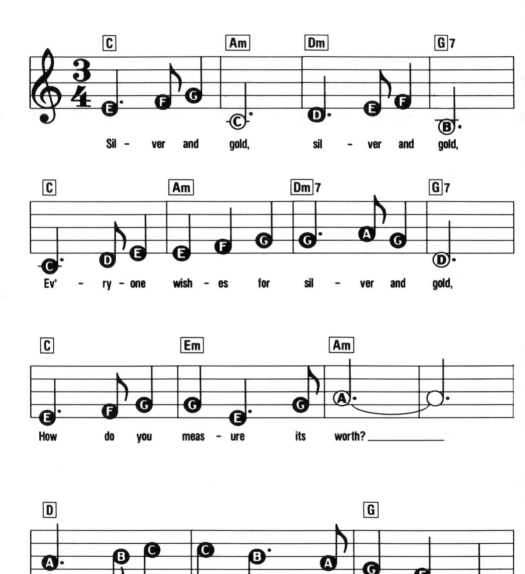

Sil - ver and gold, sil - ver and gold,

Ev' - ry - one wish - es for sil - ver and gold,

How do you meas - ure its worth? _____

Just by the pleas - ure it gives here on

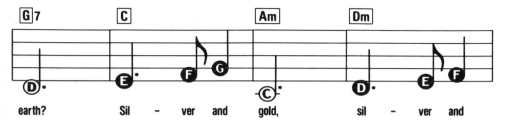

earth? Sil – ver and gold, sil – ver and

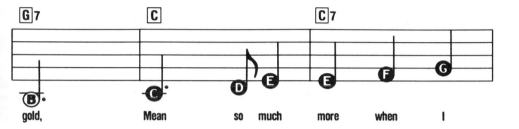

gold, Mean so much more when I

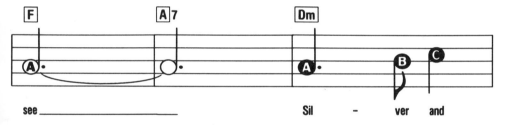

see _____ Sil – ver and

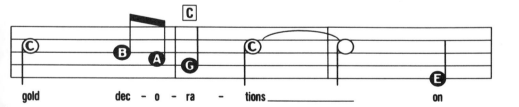

gold dec – o – ra – tions _____ on

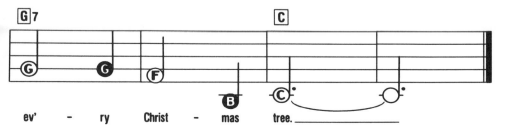

ev' – ry Christ – mas tree. _____

Silver Bells

Regi-Sound Program: 7
Rhythm: Waltz

Words and Music by Jay Livingston
and Ray Evans

Cit - y side - walks, bus - y side - walks dressed in
street lights, ev - en stop lights blink a

hol - i - day style. In the air there's a feel - ing of
bright red and green, As the shop - pers rush home with their

Christ - mas. _____ Chil - dren laugh - ing, peo - ple pass - ing, meet - ing
treas - ures. _____ Hear the snow crunch, see the kids bunch, this is

smile af - ter smile, And on ev - 'ry street cor - ner you
San - ta's big scene, And a - bove all this bus - tle you

hear: _____
hear: _____ Sil - ver bells, _____

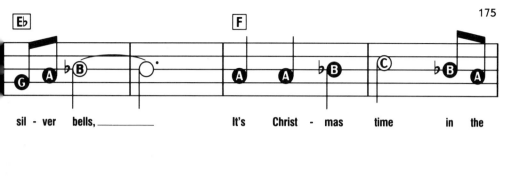

sil - ver bells, _____ It's Christ - mas time in the

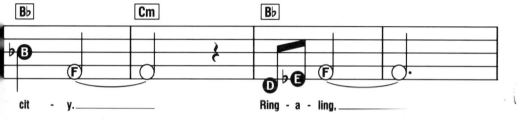

cit - y. _____ Ring - a - ling, _____

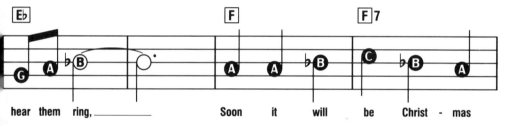

hear them ring, _____ Soon it will be Christ - mas

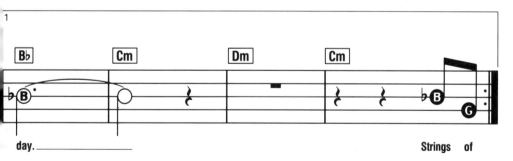

day. _____ Strings of

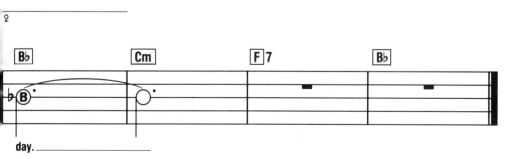

day. _____

Sleigh Ride

Words by Mitchell Parish
Music by LeRoy Anderson

Regi-Sound Program: 8
Rhythm: Fox Trot or Swing

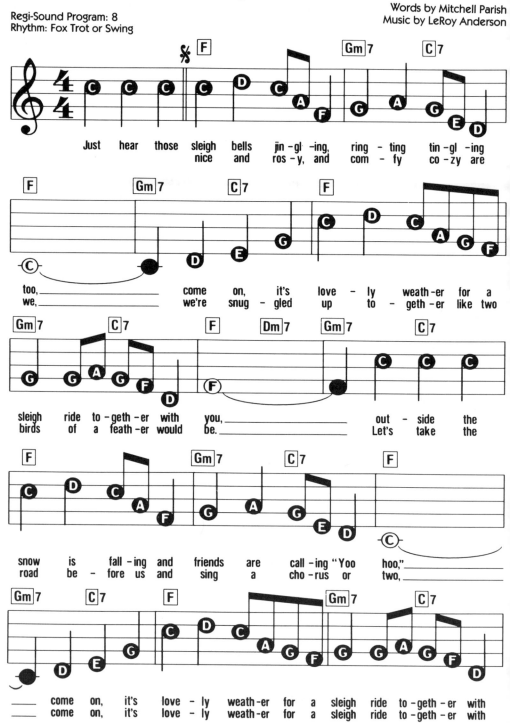

The Star Carol

Regi-Sound Program: 3
Rhythm: Waltz

Lyric by Wihla Hutson
Music by Alfred Burt

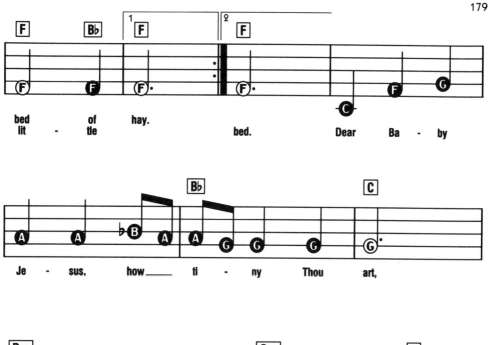

bed of hay.
lit - tle bed. Dear Ba - by

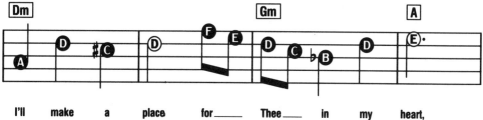

Je - sus, how___ ti - ny Thou art,

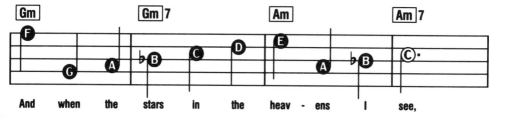

I'll make a place for___ Thee___ in my heart,

And when the stars in the heav - ens I see,

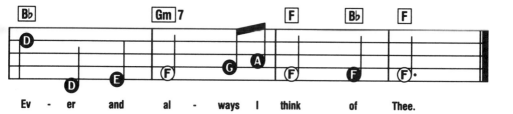

Ev - er and al - ways I think of Thee.

Suzy Snowflake

Regi-Sound Program: 2
Rhythm: Fox Trot or Swing

Words and Music by Sid Tepper
and Roy Bennett

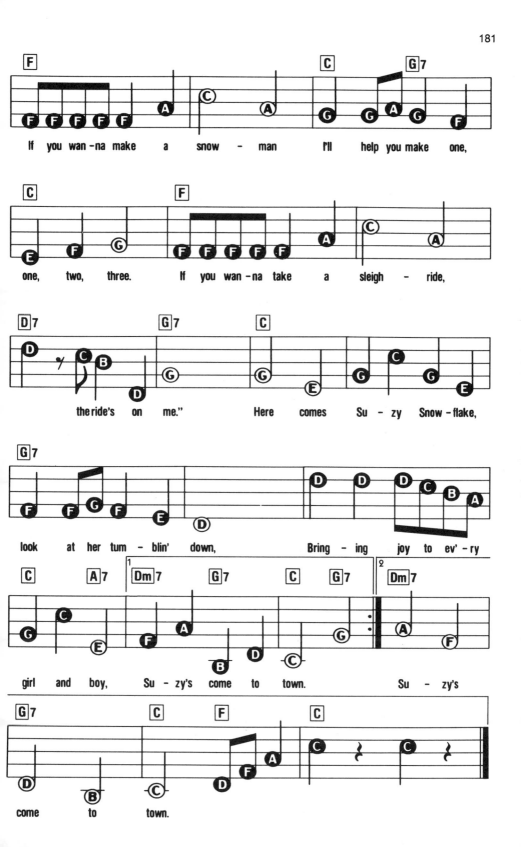

That Christmas Feeling

Regi-Sound Program: 1
Rhythm: Fox Trot or Swing

Words and Music by Bennie Benjamin
and George Weiss

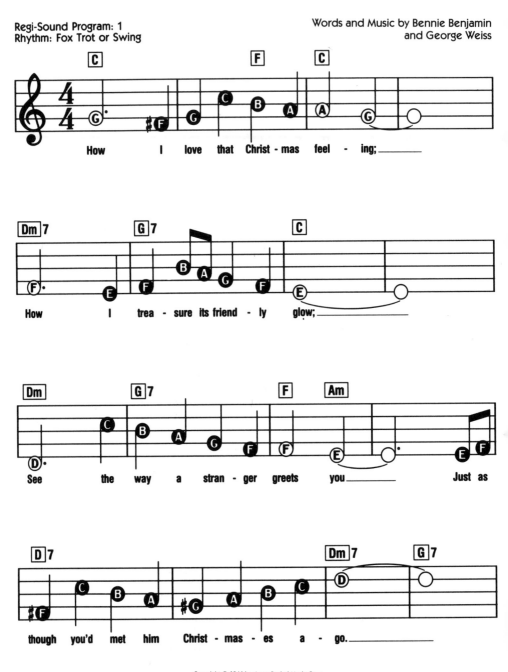

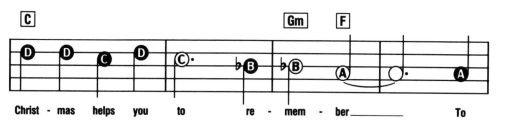

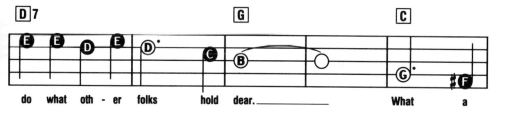

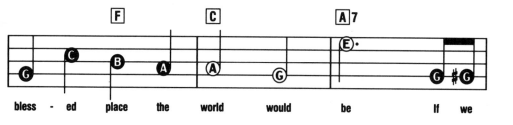

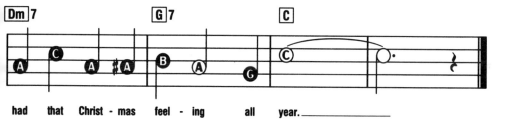

There Is No Christmas Like A Home Christmas

Regi-Sound Program: 4
Rhythm: Fox Trot or Swing

Words by Carl Sigman
Music by Mickey J. Addy

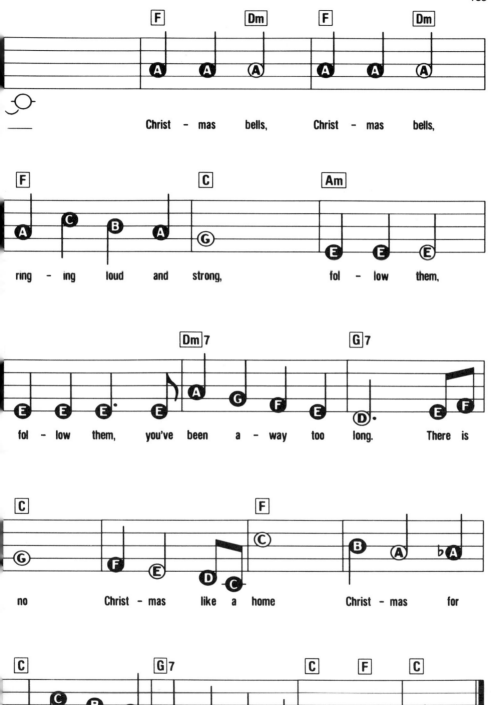

Christ - mas bells, Christ - mas bells,

ring - ing loud and strong, fol - low them,

fol - low them, you've been a - way too long. There is

no Christ - mas like a home Christ - mas for

that's the time of year all roads lead home.

Toyland

Regi-Sound Program: 4
Rhythm: Waltz

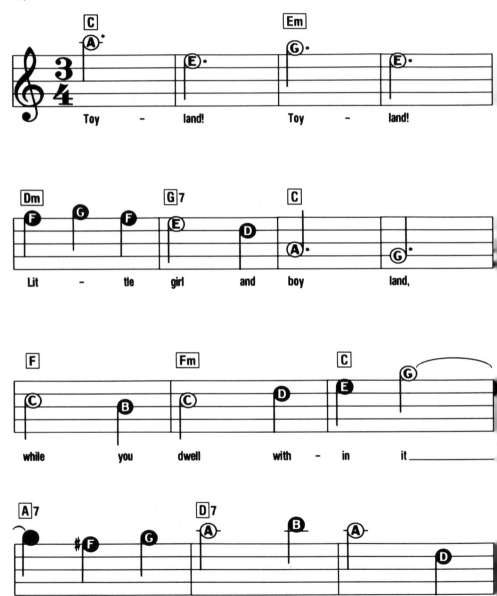

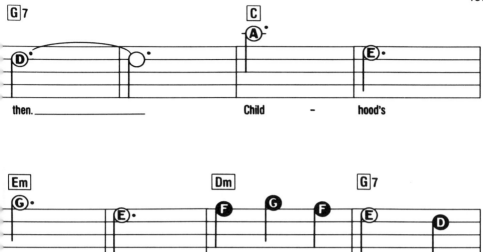

then._____ Child - hood's

toy - land, mys - tic mer - ry

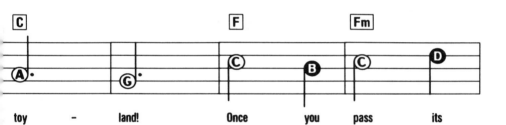

toy - land! Once you pass its

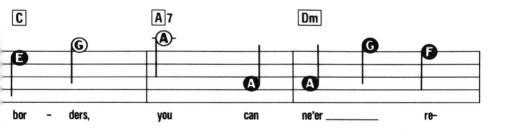

bor - ders, you can ne'er _____ re-

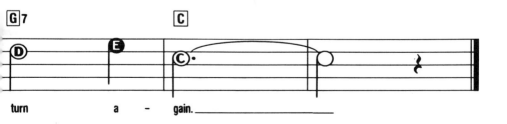

turn a - gain._____

Up On The Housetop

Regi-Sound Program: 5
Rhythm: Fox Trot

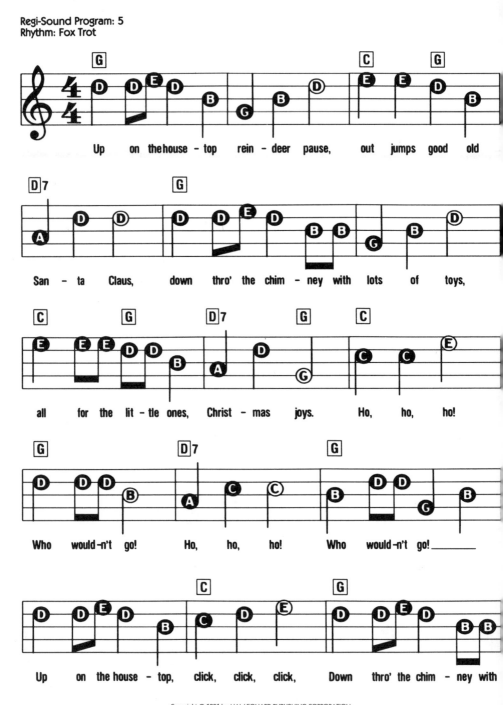

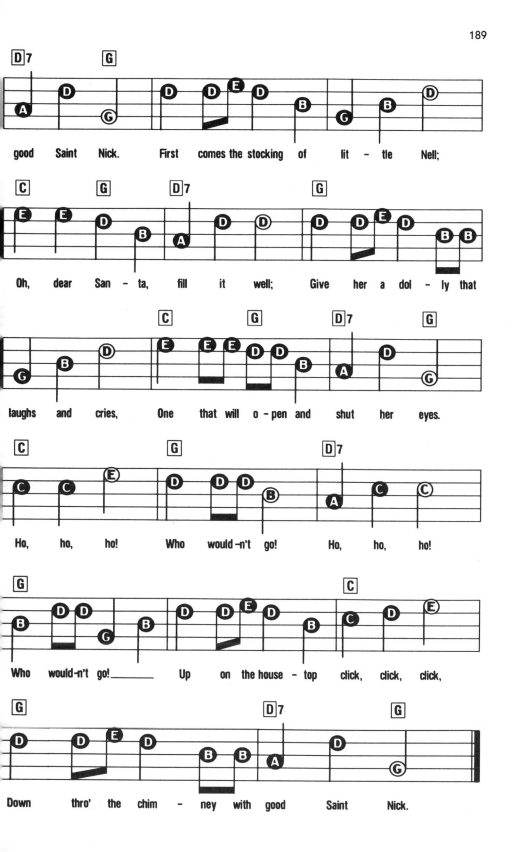

We Three Kings Of Orient Are

Regi-Sound Program: 9
Rhythm: Waltz

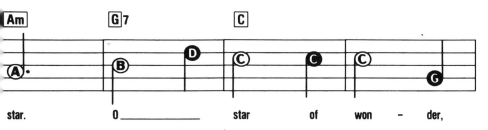

star.   O _____ star   of   won – der,

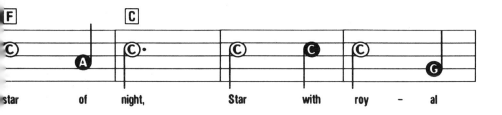

star   of   night,   Star   with   roy – al

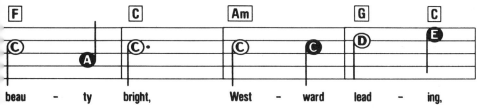

beau – ty   bright,   West – ward   lead – ing,

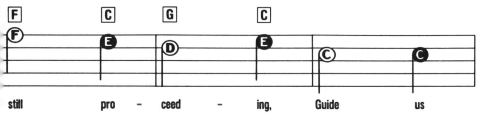

still   pro – ceed – ing,   Guide   us

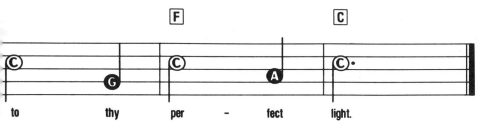

to   thy   per – fect   light.

We Wish You A Merry Christmas

Regi-Sound Program: 4
Rhythm: Waltz

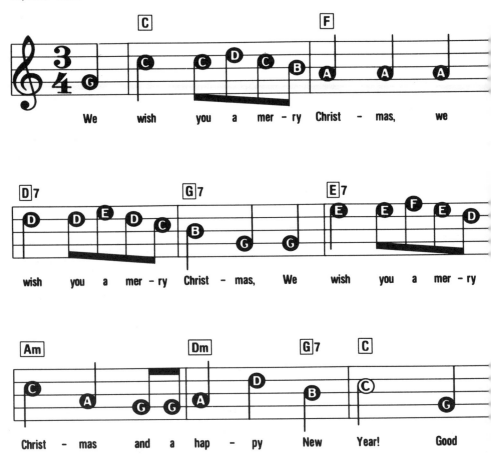

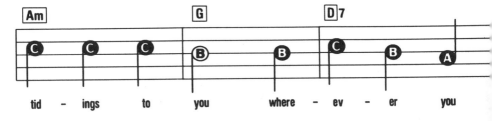

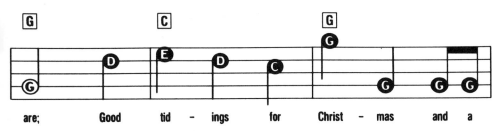

are;   Good   tid – ings   for   Christ – mas   and   a

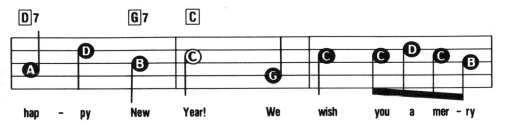

hap – py   New   Year!   We   wish   you   a   mer – ry

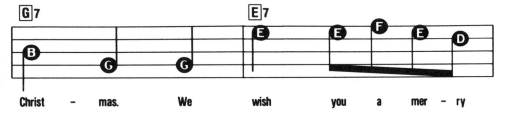

Christ – mas,   we   wish   you   a   mer – ry

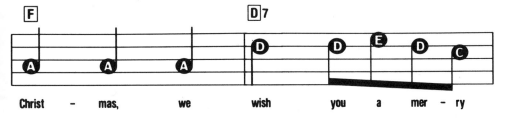

Christ – mas.   We   wish   you   a   mer – ry

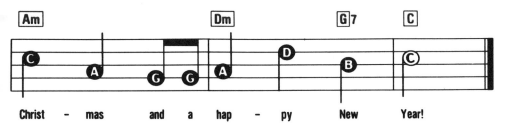

Christ – mas   and   a   hap – py   New   Year!

What Child Is This?

Regi-Sound Program: 10
Rhythm: Waltz

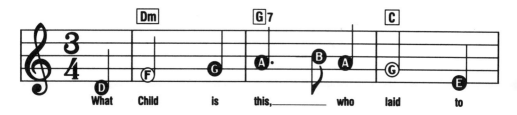

What Child is this,_____ who laid to

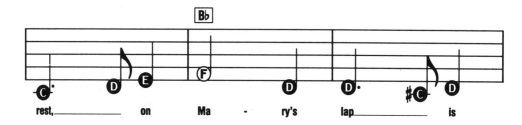

rest,_____ on Ma - ry's lap_____ is

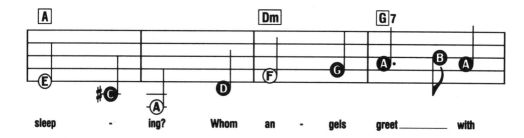

sleep - ing? Whom an - gels greet_____ with

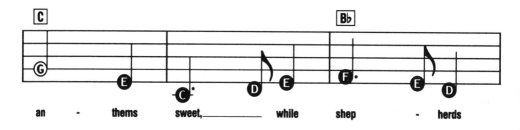

an - thems sweet,_____ while shep - herds

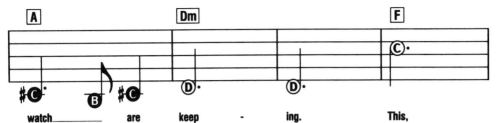

watch_____ are keep - ing. This,

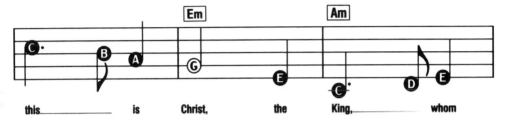

this_____ is Christ, the King,_____ whom

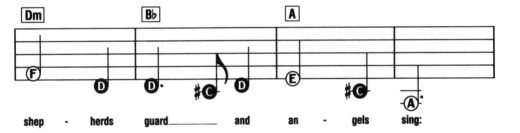

shep - herds guard_____ and an - gels sing:

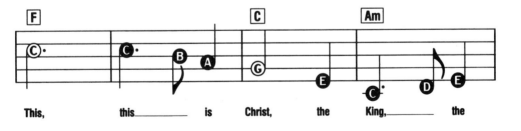

This, this_____ is Christ, the King,_____ the

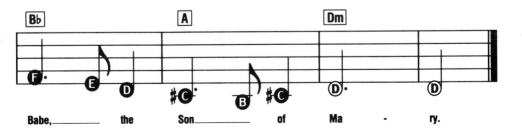

Babe,_____ the Son_____ of Ma - ry.

While Shepherds Watched Their Flocks By Night

Regi-Sound Program: 1
Rhythm: March or None

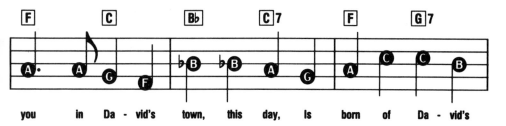

you in Da - vid's town, this day, Is born of Da - vid's

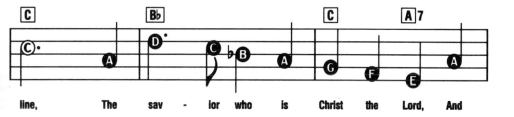

line, The sav - ior who is Christ the Lord, And

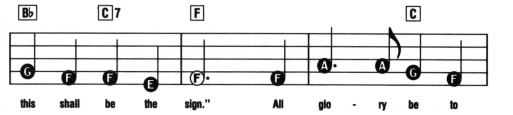

this shall be the sign." All glo - ry be to

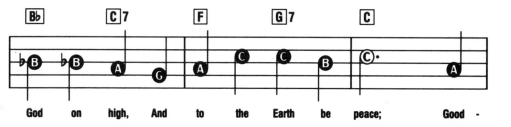

God on high, And to the Earth be peace; Good -

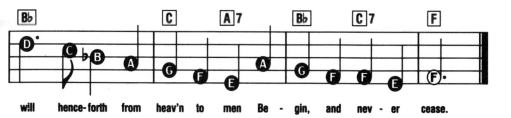

will hence-forth from heav'n to men Be - gin, and nev - er cease.

Winter Wonderland

Regi-Sound Program: 4
Rhythm: Swing

Words by Dick Smith
Music by Felix Bernard

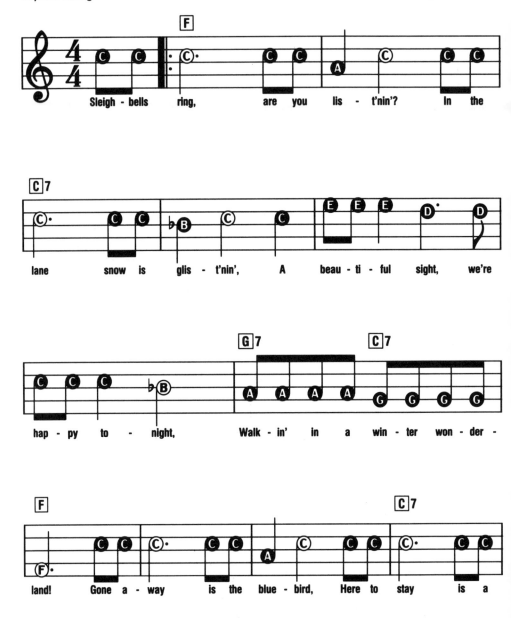

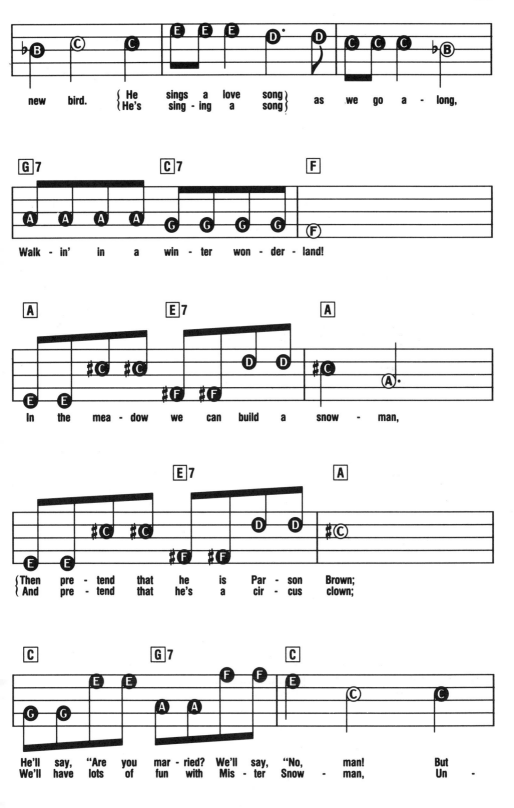

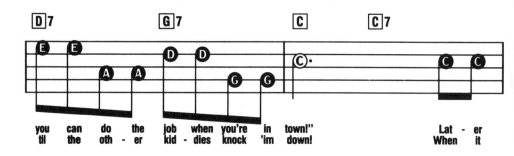

D7   **G**7   **C**   **C**7

you can do the job when you're in town!"   Lat - er
til the oth - er kid - dies knock 'im down!   When it

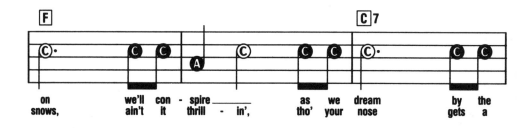

F   **C**7

on   we'll con - spire _____ as we dream by the
snows,   ain't it thrill - in', tho' your nose gets a

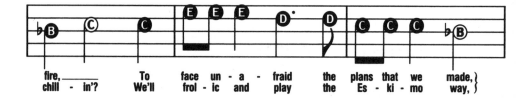

fire, _____ To face un - a - fraid the plans that we made,
chill - in'? We'll frol - ic and play the Es - ki - mo way,

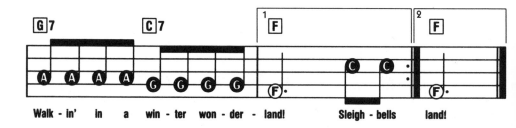

G7   **C**7   1 **F**   2 **F**

Walk - in' in a win - ter won - der - land!   Sleigh - bells land!

The Twelve Days Of Christmas

Regi-Sound Program: 5
Rhythm: None

202

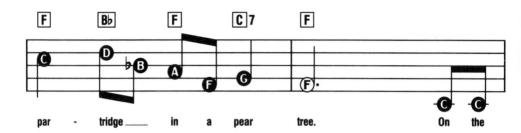

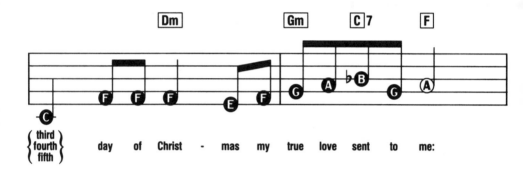

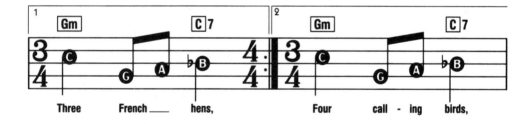

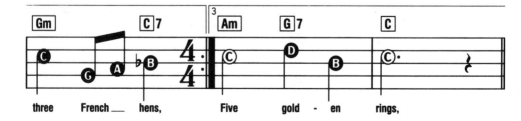

You Make It Feel Like Christmas

Regi-Sound Program: 3
Rhythm: Ballad or Slow Rock

Words and Music by
Neil Diamond

Look at us now, part of it all. In spite of it all, we're

still a-round. Lov - ers in love, just like we were.
Look at the sun shin - ing on me.
Sleep - y we are, but hap - py to - gether.

Be - ing a - part's a lone - ly sound. When peo - ple ask how
No - where could be a bet - ter place. Lov - ers in love,
Sounds of for - ev - er greet the day. So wake up the kids.

we stay to - geth - er, I say you nev - er let me down. And
that's what we are, I reach for that star out there in space. 'Cause
Put on some tea. Light up the tree. It's Christ - mas day. Yeah,

you make it feel like Christ - mas   e - ven when things go wrong.

I hear the sound of Christ - mas in your song

all year long.

long.

Light up the tree; it's Christ - mas time.

You're All I Want For Christmas

Regi-Sound Program: 3
Rhythm: Pops or 8 Beat

Words and Music by Glen Moore
and Seger Ellis

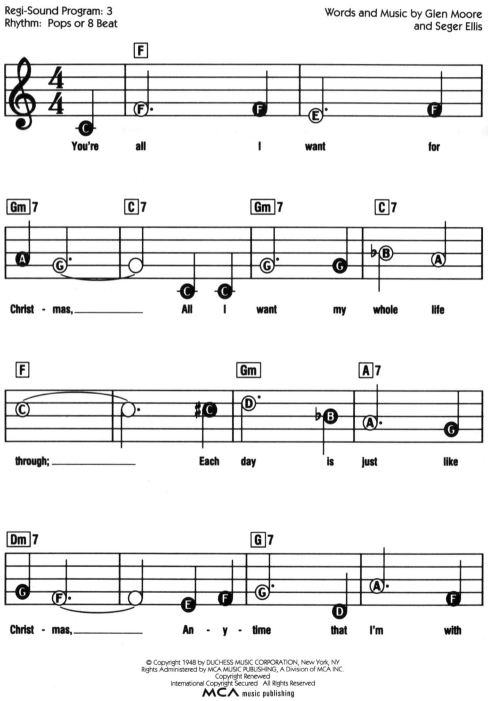

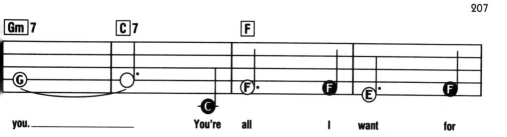

you. _____ You're all I want for

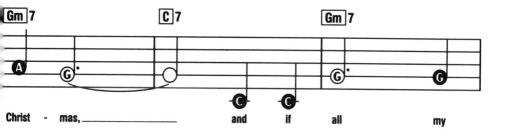

Christ - mas, _____ and if all my

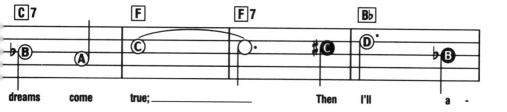

dreams come true; _____ Then I'll a -

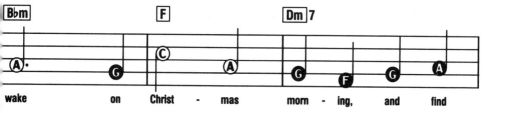

wake on Christ - mas morn - ing, and find

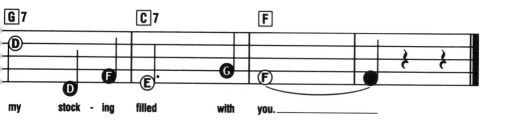

my stock - ing filled with you. _____

easy ELECTRONIC KEYBOARD MUSIC®

Regi-Sound Programs

- Match the Regi-Sound Program number on the song to the corresponding numbered category below. Select and activate an instrumental sound available on your instrument.

- Choose an automatic rhythm appropriate to the mood and style of the song. (Consult your Owner's Guide for proper operation of automatic rhythm features.)

- Adjust the tempo and volume controls to comfortable settings.

Regi-Sound Program

1	Flute, Pan Flute, Jazz Flute
2	Clarinet, Organ
3	Violin, Strings
4	Brass, Trumpet
5	Synth Ensemble, Accordion, Brass
6	Pipe Organ, Harpsichord
7	Jazz Organ, Vibraphone, Vibes, Electric Piano, Jazz Guitar
8	Piano, Electric Piano
9	Trumpet, Trombone, Clarinet, Saxophone, Oboe
10	Violin, Cello, Strings